CHOPPERS

AND CUSTOM MOTORCYCLES

Doug Mitchel

Publications International, Ltd.

Manufactured in China.

8 7 6 5 4 3 2 1

ISBN: 1-4127-1202-5

Library of Congress Control Number: 2005922658

Credits

Photographs on pages 112-115 and 228-231 by Joseph E. Mielke. Photo on page 270 by Kristina Pamias. Photos on pages 142-145 by John Mann/Chrome Pony Photography. All other photographs by Doug Mitchel.

Very special thanks to the owners of the motorcycles pictured, without whose enthusiastic cooperation this book would not have been possible.

TABLE OF CONTENTS

INTRODUCTION

They had once been the province of a small cadre of enthusiasts, but choppers have since hit the big time. Thanks in large part to exposure on national television and cable shows, their combination of sight and sound has made them the equivalent of mobile celebrities.

But choppers as a breed are really not new. In fact, they can trace their heritage to the late 1940s, when surplus military bikes were stripped of unnecessary parts and given homemade paint jobs to become "Bobbers." Bikes sprouting extended forks, stepped saddles, tall sissy bars, and wild paint schemes appeared in the late '60s as "Choppers," and the die was cast.

Today, choppers take many different forms. *Old School* bikes favor the minimalist styling of Bobbers, *Early Choppers* the look of their original namesakes. *Factory and Factory Modified* customs from relatively small companies can be purchased right off the showroom floor, while *Radicals* are ornate rides that can take many months—and dollars—to build. *Pro Street* bikes lean toward performance,

and choppers that fall through the categorical cracks can be termed *Special Construction*. In some cases, bikes employ traits of more than one class, making them difficult to place—though we've tried to anyway.

Custom bikes tend to incorporate fascinating details that aren't obvious from 50 feet away, so each bike is given four pages of photos to strut its stuff. Entries are accompanied by a specification chart listing dimensions and features, and a glossary in the back of the book explains some of the terms used in the spec charts and descriptions.

Many books and television shows have highlighted bikes from the big-name, high-volume builders. What's focused on here are choppers built by lesser-known but equally talented shops and individuals, most of whom produce only a handful of machines a year—and often come up with truly fascinating creations. These bikes provide a look not only at where the chopper phenomenon came from, but also where it's heading. We hope you enjoy the trip.

First appearing in the 1960s and 1970s, early choppers typically carried long forks, stepped "King and Queen" seats, and wild paint jobs. Most were based on Harley-Davidsons, British twins, or Honda's 750 Four. Later models sported *really* long forks, along with tall sissy bars and "ape hanger" handlebars. So popular were these choppers that many recent builds mimic their decades-old styling themes.

Early Choppers

The Beast

When Honda introduced its four-cylinder CB750 for 1969, the motorcycle world took notice. That included the faction known to take perfectly good bikes and turn them into something their own designers wouldn't recognize. And so it was that shortly after hitting American soil, Japan's new superbike became the basis for a new breed of chopper.

The owner of this bike remembers those days well, though he was just a lad at the time. After he grew up, he wanted to build a machine that reminded him of those wondrous choppers he remembered from his youth.

A custom-built hardtail frame was mated with a long set of springer forks to create a radically stretched chassis. Classic Invader wheels were added at each end, only the rear hosting a brake—and a rather feeble drum brake at that. The 736-cc (45-cubic-inch) four-cylinder engine was treated to a set of Mikuni carburetors and Fubar 4-into-2 exhaust system. A fuel tank specially fabricated for this machine hosts flames on top of the black paint that was applied to all the metal-work.

While it's a modern cre-ation, this Honda-powered chopper accurately follows the trail blazed by its ances-tors, which also blazed a vivid memory in a young enthusiast's mind.

The Beast

SPECIFICATIONS

Owner: Keith Barnett

Builder: Lowriders by
Summers/
Slicks Choppers

Model: The Beast

Frame: Santee, 9 up, 10 out

Forks: AEE, springer,
21 inches over

Rake: 42 degrees

Rear susp.: Hardtail

Front wheel: Invader, 19-inch

Front brake: None

Rear wheel: Invader, 16-inch

Rear brake: Drum

Rear tire: 130 mm

Engine: 45-cubic-inch Honda

Exhaust: Fubar

Trans.: Honda, 5-speed

Paint by: Lowriders by
Summers

The long tank was specially made to cover the radically stretched top tube of the custom-built frame. It's dressed in period flames.

Below: At the time of its introduction, Honda's 750-cc inline four was among the most potent motorcycle engines available, and velvety smooth to boot; as such, it was a natural for customizers. This one wears a 4-into-2 exhaust header that was a common replacement in the day.

Opposite page, bottom: While the Honda 750 came standard with a massive front disc brake—comforting, considering its speed potential—this chopper has no front brake at all and only a rear drum brake to slow it down. Cast-spoke Invader wheels were a 70's chopper mainstay.

FLH

year: 1958
builder: Jerry Morgan
class: Early Chopper

Aside from a cherry Early Chopper, what we see here is a study in perseverance; owner Jerry Morgan first customized this 1958 Harley-Davidson FLH in 1969, and has redone it five times since.

In 1971, after undergoing a second "build," the bike was wrecked almost beyond repair. But repair it Jerry did—making it even better than it was before. And that's been the story with each overhaul that has brought it to this, its sixth incarnation.

By now, there is little left of the original 1958 Harley. The frame has been converted to a hardtail configuration, the forks exchanged for an extended girder setup. The engine, while still true to its Panhead design, has been modified for added power and durability; chief among its revisions are a Weber two-barrel carburetor and Alphabet headers. A custom-made fuel tank and classic Invader wheels substitute for the original pieces.

Most obvious among the alterations, however, is the contemporary "chameleon" paint, which looks purple, green, or a combination of both, depending on the angle of view. It represents one of the many improvements made to the bike since its first round of customization back in 1969. And while it appears to have finally reached perfection, one wonders if it's truly "finished."

Opposite page: Fuel tank and frame wear modern "chameleon" paint that flops from green to purple when viewed from different angles.

Above: Harley-Davidson Panhead V-twin was given many updates, including an unusual two-barrel Weber carburetor conversion, with its long intake manifold and mesh air cleaner.

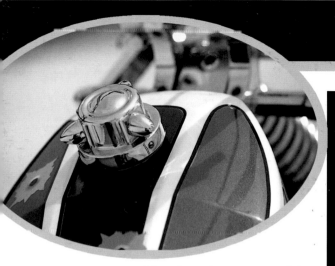

Note how the contours of the frame have been smoothed and molded to perfection.

SPECIFICATIONS

Owner: Jerry Morgan

Builder: Jerry Morgan

Model: FLH

Frame: Harley-Davidson

Forks: EME, girder, 14 inches over

Rake: 46 degrees

Rear susp.: Hardtail

Front wheel: Invader, 19-inch

Front brake: Drum

Rear wheel: Invader, 16-inch

Rear tire: 130 mm

Rear brake: Drum

Engine: 74-cubic-inch Harley-Davidson

Exhaust: Joe Alphabet

Trans.: Harley-Davidson, 4-speed

Paint by: Jerry Morgan

Outlaw

year: 1968
builder: Matthew Tomas
class: Early Chopper

Originally built in the 1970s, this Triumph Bonneville chopper was left for dead before being located by the current owner. Once acquired, the machine was treated to a complete restoration.

Changes to the original 650-cc (40-cubic-inch) vertical-twin engine were limited to the addition of a "drag-pipe" exhaust. The forward part of the frame is stock, but the swingarm and shocks were removed and replaced by steel tubing, converting it to a hardtail. Girder forks were fitted in place of the original telescopics. A 16-inch spoke wheel with drum brake holds up the rear, while the 21-inch spoke in front has no brake at all.

Part of the restoration included a fresh coat of purple paint with classic yellow flames. The scheme is similar to what was originally applied in the 1970s, making this chopper a bit of history brought back to life.

Outlaw

Above: The two-cylinder Triumph engine was known as the Classic British twin, and many powered choppers of the 1970s. This example is fitted with a "drag pipe" exhaust. ***Opposite page, top:*** Flamed paint job mimics that originally applied to this chopper in the '70s. Note the "spired" gas cap, another throwback to its origins. ***Bottom:*** Most Triumphs of the '60s came with a chromed rear fender, and that theme is echoed here—though the original was much longer.

SPECIFICATIONS

Owner: Matthew Tomas

Builder: Matthew Tomas

Model: Outlaw

Frame: Triumph

Forks: Girder

Rake: 40 degrees

Rear susp.: Hardtail

Front wheel: Spoke, 21-inch

Front brake: None

Rear wheel: Spoke, 16-inch

Rear tire: 130 mm

Rear brake: Drum

Engine: 40-cubic-inch Triumph

Exhaust: Jireh

Trans.: Triumph, 4-speed

Paint by: Phil Brenneman

Cherry Chopper

year: 1978
builder: Terry Douglas
class: Early Chopper

Like many early customs, the Cherry Chopper started life as a Harley-Davidson; in this case, a 1978 FXE that was purchased new by the current owner. This model combined the frame and engine of the big FL touring bikes with the lighter forks and hooded headlight of the XL Sportster.

Extended forks were a chopper staple back then, and these have been stretched ten inches and mounted at a 40-degree rake. Without a stretched downtube, the longer forks lift the whole chassis off the ground, placing the front higher than the back—another trait common to early choppers. Other elements that defined the breed are also present: midrise handlebars, stepped saddle, and straight pipes.

Whether new or old, what often sets one chopper apart from another is the paint scheme, and the Cherry Chopper is no exception. Its deep Cherry Red basecoat was treated to swirling gold graphics that dressed the tank, rear fender, and frame. While the design is typical of the 1970s, the quality and detailing benefit from modern techniques—giving this bike a look few of its ancestors could match.

21

Cherry Chopper

Stretched forks, midrise handlebars, stepped seat, and straight pipes make this example representative of the typical chopper of the 1970s. What sets it apart is the paint scheme, which is more elaborate than most of the period.

SPECIFICATIONS

Owner: Terry Douglas

Builder: Terry Douglas

Model: Cherry Chopper

Frame: Harley-Davidson

Forks: Harley-Davidson, telescopic, 10 inches over

Rake: 40 degrees

Rear susp.: Swingarm

Front wheel: Spoke, 21-inch

Front brake: Harley-Davidson, dual disc

Rear wheel: Spoke, 16-inch

Rear tire: 130 mm

Rear brake: Harley-Davidson, disc

Engine: 80-cubic-inch Harley-Davidson

Exhaust: Paughco

Trans.: Harley-Davidson, 4-speed

Paint by: Spencer

Mississippi Queen

Although assembled using a lot of Harley-Davidson components, this bike was never a complete Harley to begin with. For one thing, the builder wanted certain features the Milwaukee company never offered to the public.

Primary among those features were the front and rear suspension systems. Hardtail frames were the traditional choice, but they were uncomfortable over bumps. So a Jammer frame was chosen that incorporated a plunger-type rear suspension—similar to that used on old Indian motorcycles—providing a bit of cushioned wheel travel. In front, girder forks have a one-piece design, but move up and down on pivoting links.

Harley-Davidson did, however, supply the drivetrain: a 74-cubic-inch "Shovelhead" V-twin and 4-speed transmission. A two-into-one header from Cycle Shack helps the old engine breathe. Power routes to a stock Harley spoke wheel with drum brake; in front, a Hallcraft 21-inch spoke wheel with disc brake was chosen for more of a "chopper" look.

The fuel tank is set back on the frame's top tube, allowing space for a graphics panel carrying the bike's Mississippi Queen moniker. A set of nearly flat drag bars in tandem with a deeply contoured "King and Queen" seat add an appropriate look to a bike built in the Early Chopper style—which was something never offered by the folks from Milwaukee.

25

Mississippi Queen

SPECIFICATIONS

Owner: Tony Zizzo

Builder: Tony Zizzo/
Zizzo Racing

Model: Mississippi Queen

Frame: Jammer

Forks: Springer,
6 inches over

Rake: 42 degrees

Rear susp.: Plunger

Front wheel: Hallcraft, 21-inch

Front brake: Disc

Rear wheel: Harley-Davidson,
16-inch

Rear tire: 130 mm

Rear brake: Drum

Engine: 74-cubic-inch
Harley-Davidson

Exhaust: Cycle Shack

Trans.: Harley-Davidson,
4-speed

Paint by: Tony Zizzo

A stepped King and Queen seat is an Early Chopper mainstay, a signature of the breed.

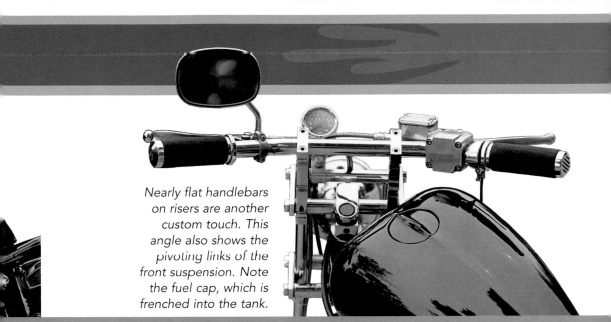

Nearly flat handlebars on risers are another custom touch. This angle also shows the pivoting links of the front suspension. Note the fuel cap, which is frenched into the tank.

One of the more interesting aspects of the Mississippi Queen is the suspension system. In front, solid girder forks ride up and down on short, pivoting links at the top. A large coil spring supplies cushioning, but without the aid of a shock absorber, tends to give a bouncy ride. Same goes for the rear plunger-type suspension. Its advantage is that it looks like a hardtail frame, but supplies at least a little wheel travel—and that's better than none at all.

Captain America

It's perhaps the best-known chopper in the world, and to many, the Captain America bike from the film *Easy Rider* defines the breed.

The bike shown is not a replica; it is one of two identical choppers originally built by Cliff Vaughn for use in *Easy Rider*. This is the one that was wrecked at the end of the film. The other was reportedly stolen, likely sold for parts by a thief unaware of its significance.

After the filming, the wrecked bike was procured by actor Dan Haggerty, who began rebuilding it but never finished. It was then sold, the restoration being completed by Dave Ohrt. The owner, who wishes to remain anonymous, has graciously loaned it to the National Motorcycle Museum in Anamosa, Iowa, where it is currently on display.

year: 1969
builder: Cliff Vaughn/Dave Ohrt
class: Early Chopper

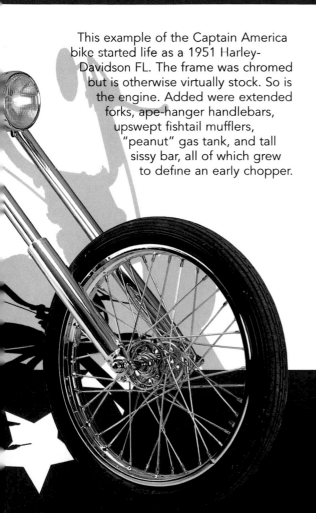

This example of the Captain America bike started life as a 1951 Harley-Davidson FL. The frame was chromed but is otherwise virtually stock. So is the engine. Added were extended forks, ape-hanger handlebars, upswept fishtail mufflers, "peanut" gas tank, and tall sissy bar, all of which grew to define an early chopper.

SPECIFICATIONS

Owner: On display at National Motorcycle Museum

Builder: Cliff Vaughn/Dave Ohrt

Model: Captain America

Frame: Harley-Davidson

Forks: Telescopic, 12 inches over

Rake: 42 degrees

Rear susp.: Hardtail

Front wheel: Spoke, 21-inch

Front brake: none

Rear wheel: Spoke, 16-inch

Rear tire: 120 mm

Rear brake: Harley-Davidson, drum

Engine: 74-cubic-inch Harley-Davidson

Exhaust: Cliff Vaughn

Trans.: Harley-Davidson, 4-speed

Paint by: Cliff Vaughn

Captain America

Below: People from around the world recognize the Stars and Stripes paint scheme of Captain America's fuel tank.

Above: Fishtail mufflers were popular in the 1950s, and add a nostalgic touch to the upswept exhaust. The chrome rear fender is from a Triumph; the seat buttons from a '64 Chevrolet. Opposite page: Easy Rider, starring Dennis Hopper (left) and Peter Fonda (driving the Captain America bike), was released in 1969, and soon became a cult classic.

Fashioned after Bobbers of the late 1940s and '50s that were often built from stripped military surplus bikes, Old School choppers put an emphasis on lean and mean. Engines typically are—or mimic—older Harley-Davidson V-twins. Hot Rods of the period also lend an influence, so the bikes have a simple, retro look generally devoid of the stretched proportions and forced sheetmetal of many other choppers.

Old School

Shovel

year: 1974
builder: Dragon's
class: Old School

34

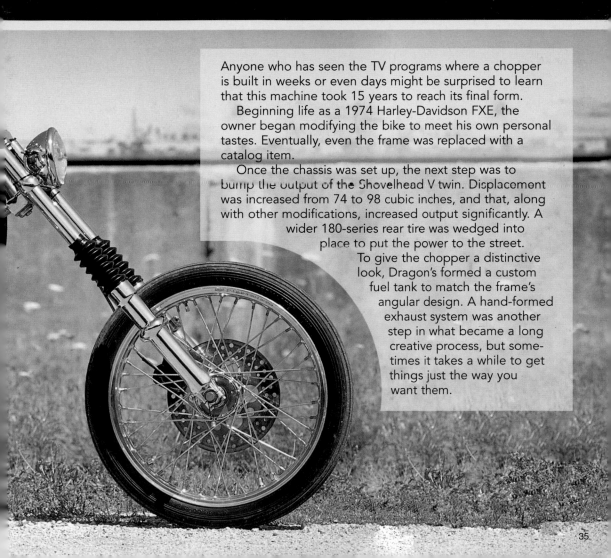

Anyone who has seen the TV programs where a chopper is built in weeks or even days might be surprised to learn that this machine took 15 years to reach its final form.

Beginning life as a 1974 Harley-Davidson FXE, the owner began modifying the bike to meet his own personal tastes. Eventually, even the frame was replaced with a catalog item.

Once the chassis was set up, the next step was to bump the output of the Shovelhead V twin. Displacement was increased from 74 to 98 cubic inches, and that, along with other modifications, increased output significantly. A wider 180-series rear tire was wedged into place to put the power to the street.

To give the chopper a distinctive look, Dragon's formed a custom fuel tank to match the frame's angular design. A hand-formed exhaust system was another step in what became a long creative process, but some-times it takes a while to get things just the way you want them.

Shovel

The Harley-Davidson Shovelhead engine was given a big boost in displacement—and power. Note the milled valve covers and custom-bent exhaust pipes with their Maltese-cross emblems.

Opposite page: Handmade fuel tank with its rounded leading edge took some time to make. Note the fuel petcock's placement at the rear of the tank, where it's handy.

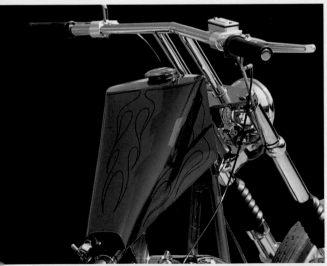

SPECIFICATIONS

Owner: Greg Ponto

Builder: Dragon's

Model: Shovel

Frame: Mid-USA, 3 up, 1 out

Forks: Harley-Davidson, telescopic, 4 inches over

Rake: Stock

Rear susp.: Hardtail

Front wheel: Spoke, 21-inch

Front brake: Disc

Rear wheel: Spoke, 16-inch

Rear tire: 180 mm

Rear brake: Disc

Engine: 98-cubic-inch Harley-Davidson

Exhaust: Dragon's

Trans.: Harley-Davidson 4-speed

Paint by: Helicopter Eddie

As a prime example of the Old School chopper, Robert Berry's bike shuns the normal sculpted metal, billet trim, and big-inch engine of most customs, relying instead on a bare-bones look and hardware with historical significance.

Chief among these is the engine: a tried-and-true 74-cubic-inch Harley-Davidson Knucklehead, which is all stock save for the turned-up Paughco exhaust system. Granted, the frame is a modern item—a Paughco with 3-inch downtube stretch—but the springer forks are very close to those that supported Harleys in the early postwar years.

Of course, this wouldn't be much of a custom without a few nonstock components, but most are anchored in tradition. The fuel tank carries the classic teardrop shape, the rear fender is a cut-down version of the original Harley piece, and the overall look pays homage to 1950s Bobbers. Choppers of the 1960s and 1970s inspired the ape-hanger handlebars, a common item on many great Old School bikes.

SPECIFICATIONS

Owner: Robert Berry

Builder: Psycle Barn/Rodney Mann/Robert Berry

Model: EL

Frame: Paughco, 3 up

Forks: Springer, 4 inches over

Rake: 34 degrees

Rear susp.: Hardtail

Front wheel: CCI spoke, 21-inch

Front brake: Harley-Davidson, drum

Rear wheel: CCI spoke, 16-inch

Rear tire: 140 mm

Rear brake: GMA, disc

Engine: 74-cubic-inch Harley-Davidson

Exhaust: Paughco

Trans.: Harley-Davidson, 4-speed

Paint by: Rodney Mann

Below, left: You can't get more classic in the powerplant department than a Harley-Davidson Knucklehead. That's not Harley's term for it, by the way; the nickname was coined by riders, because the large bolts on the valve covers look like knuckles on a fist. And in its day, the Knucklehead packed a pretty good punch. *Right:* Springer forks of this style first appeared on Harleys in the late 1920s. They've reappeared on modern versions. *Below, right:* Turned-up exhaust pipes were a fixture on early choppers. The original Harley drum brake may suffice up front, but the rear wheel hosts a modern disc.

Almost by definition, Old School choppers take the lean and mean approach, with little in the way of fancy trim. Fancy paint, however, is OK.

Unlike some Old School choppers, this one really is old—with a few exceptions.

A restored-to-stock 1941 Harley-Davidson flathead would be a valuable piece, but Robert Berry is a chopper guy. And he wanted to add a flathead to his stable to keep his chopped 1947 Harley Knucklehead company.

A 1941 Harley-Davidson Model U formed the basis for his flathead chopper. For the most part, the original hardware was retained: a low-compression 74-cubic-inch V-twin, four-speed transmission, hardtail frame, springer forks, and solo saddle with sprung seat post. While a modern hand-clutch/foot-shift arrangement replaces the original foot clutch/hand shift, stock Harley drum brakes are used front and rear, each supporting classic spoked rims.

From there, customization followed a Bobber theme. The fuel tank was modified to hold gas in the left half, oil in the right, thus eliminating the separate oil tank beneath the seat. The front fender is a mere sliver of its former self, and the trimmed rear fender hosts a 1950s-era custom tail-light. Only the TT-style exhaust with its tapered-cone mufflers and the artful scalloped paint treatment give this away as a modern machine—because old-time Bobbers never looked this good.

SPECIFICATIONS

Owner: Robert Berry
Builder: Robert Berry
Model: U
Frame: Harley-Davidson
Forks: Harley-Davidson, springer
Rake: 28 degrees
Rear susp.: Hardtail
Front wheel: Harley-Davidson spoke, 19-inch
Front brake: Harley-Davidson, drum
Rear wheel: Harley-Davidson spoke, 16-inch
Rear Tire: 130 mm
Rear brake: Harley-Davidson, drum
Engine: 74-cubic-inch Harley-Davidson
Exhaust: Robert Berry
Trans.: Harley-Davidson, 4-speed
Paint by: Rodney Mann

Model U

Above: A "baloney" taillight is a 1950s styling element that still looks good today. *Above, right:* The replica horn carries a personalized touch. *Right:* Harley's classic tank-mounted instrument panel originated in the 1930s. The basic design is still used today, but many feel the old ones were more stylish.

Old Skool

year: 2004
build ███ cooter Shooterz
class: Old School

Harkening back to the early days of chopper building, Old Skool caters to the simpler design elements found on machines from the 1960s. There's little here that doesn't need to be; even the paintwork is uncharacteristically subtle.

Front to rear, Old Skool is a study in basic black. Even the exhaust pipes are wrapped in heat-insulating black tape. Only the red wheels and isolated bits of chrome and polished metal deviate from the theme, adding just the right accents. Tall handlebars and extended springer forks raked at 40 degrees add a radical element to the old-world mix.

Powering the Old Skool is a Harley-Davidson Shovelhead V-twin bumped to 93 cubic inches via S&S internal components. The 5-speed transmission is stirred by a hand shifter topped with a billiard ball—another "old" touch for the new machine.

46

Old Skool

Opposite page, top: The Harley-Davidson Shovelhead engine adds a 1960s look to this 2000s bike. Note the tape-wrapped exhaust pipes. *Bottom:* "Crazy 8" shift ball is another sixties cue.

SPECIFICATIONS

Owner: Kit Defever

Builder: Scooter Shooterz

Model: Old Skool

Frame: Paughco, 4 up, 4 out

Forks: Springer,
10 inches over

Rake: 40 degrees

Rear susp.: Hardtail

Front wheel: Spoke, 21-inch

Front brake: Drum

Rear wheel: Spoke, 18-inch

Rear tire: 180 mm

Rear brake: Exile, disc/sprocket

Engine: 93-cubic-inch
Harley-Davidson

Exhaust: Scooter Shooterz

Trans.: 5-speed, hand shift

Paint by: Scooter Shooterz

Board Track Replica

Gene Williams doesn't work out of a large production facility, nor does he have the latest machinery on hand. What he does have is an intimate knowledge of motorcycles and the know-how to assemble his own creations.

Board-track racing (so named because the oval tracks were made of wooden planks) was popular in the early days of motorcycling as a test of both speed and endurance. To build this replica of a 1930s board-track racer, Williams started with a Harley-Davidson Knucklehead engine that he bored out and fitted with a high-performance cam and dual carburetors. A 1931 Harley VL model donated its frame, which had to be stretched by an inch to fit the larger engine. (The VL came with a flathead V-twin, which is more compact—but far less powerful—than the overhead-valve Knucklehead.)

The fuel tank has been modified to carry gas only in the left half; the right half is just a cover that conceals the oil tank, battery, and ignition coil. Olive Drab paint that mimics the color used on Harleys from the late teens to the early 1930s gives the bike a period appearance—which is the whole idea.

SPECIFICATIONS

Owner: Gene Williams

Builder: Gene Williams

Model: Board Track Replica

Frame: Hardtail, 1 up

Forks: Harley-Davidson, springer

Rake: 28 degrees

Rear susp.: Hardtail

Front wheel: Harley-Davidson spoke, 21-inch

Front brake: none

Rear wheel: Harley-Davidson spoke, 21-inch

Rear brake: Harley-Davidson, drum

Engine: 61-cubic-inch Harley-Davidson

Exhaust: Gene Williams

Trans.: Harley-Davidson, hand shift

Paint by: Gene Williams

Above: Harley-Davidsons of the '30s had a hand-shift transmission and foot-operated clutch—as does this board-track replica. There's also no front brake, so the only handlebar control is for the throttle, leaving the bars devoid of levers.

Board Track Replica

Board-track racers of the 1930s typically had no brakes and certainly no lights; being a street-legal bike, this replica has both, though there's a brake only on the rear wheel. The Knucklehead engine got its name from the large valve-cover bolts that looked like knuckles on a fist. A kick-start lever stands tall next to the rear exhaust pipe; 1930s Harleys didn't have electric start, and neither does this bike.

The springer front fork is a period Harley piece. The Knucklehead engine has been modified with two carburetors instead of one, along with exhaust pipes that exit on both sides of the bike; the front cylinder to the left, the rear cylinder to the right. The tall shift lever for the transmission can be seen culminating in a knob at the rear of the fuel tank; the foot-activated clutch pedal is mounted ahead of the footpeg.

David Buerer has never been accused of being timid, so when he set out to build his own radical Old School chopper, nothing was considered out of bounds.

A Daytec hardtail frame holds lengthy 32-inch-over telescopic forks at a radical 54-degree rake; you don't need to look at the photos to tell that results in a pretty wild profile. Sixty-spoke wheels were used on both axles, as were disc brakes by Performance Machine.

Powering the Tramp is a V-twin made from after-market parts but built to resemble a classic Harley-Davidson Shovelhead engine. It displaces a healthy 93 cubic inches and wears a pair of exhaust pipes bent by Dave himself.

A fuel tank from Mid-USA was stretched to fit the frame's unusual dimensions, and painted matte black to fit David's unusual vision. And the way Tramp turned out, nobody can say that vision was too timid.

Tramp

Above: Though it resembles a 74-cubic-inch Harley-Davidson Shovelhead V-twin from the 1970s, this engine displaces 93 cubic inches and is built from modern components, including Delkron cases and S&S heads. Its short, tape-wrapped exhaust pipes were made by the owner. *Opposite page:* Virtually everything that isn't chromed has been given a matte-black finish, a fairly common combination on Old School designs. But the steeply raked forks, modern headlight, low handlebars, wraparound front fender, two-tone solo saddle, and wide rear tire leave Tramp straddling the line between Old School and Radical choppers.

SPECIFICATIONS

Owner: David Buerer

Builder: David Buerer

Model: Tramp

Frame: Daytec, 8 up, 5 out

Forks: Forks by Frank, telescopic, 32 inches over

Rake: 54 degrees

Rear susp.: Hardtail

Front wheel: Spoke, 21-inch

Front brake: Performance Machine, disc

Rear wheel: Spoke, 18-inch

Rear tire: 200 mm

Rear brake: Performance Machine, disc

Engine: 93-cubic-inch Delkron/S&S

Exhaust: David Buerer

Trans.: Jim's 5-speed

Paint by: Paint Spot

The Hobo

year: 2003
builder: Klock Werks
class: Old School

SPECIFICATIONS

Owner: Dan Cheeseman

Builder: Klock Werks

Model: The Hobo

Frame: Klock Werks

Forks: Harley-Davidson, telescopic, 2 inches under

Rake: 28 degrees

Rear susp.: Hardtail

Front wheel: Spoke, 19-inch

Front brake: None

Rear wheel: Spoke, 17-inch

Rear tire: 190 mm

Rear brake: Exile disc/sprocket

Engine: 88-cubic-inch Rev Tech

Exhaust: Klock Werks

Trans.: Harley-Davidson, 4-speed, hand shift

Paint by: Klock Werks

The Hobo is aptly named, as its assorted bits and pieces were collected from many sources over a two-year period. All the adopted parts, which include Schwinn bicycle handgrips and a throttle from a jet ski, were assembled with only a rough idea of the desired outcome; many others, such as the fender brackets and handlebars, were handmade by the builder.

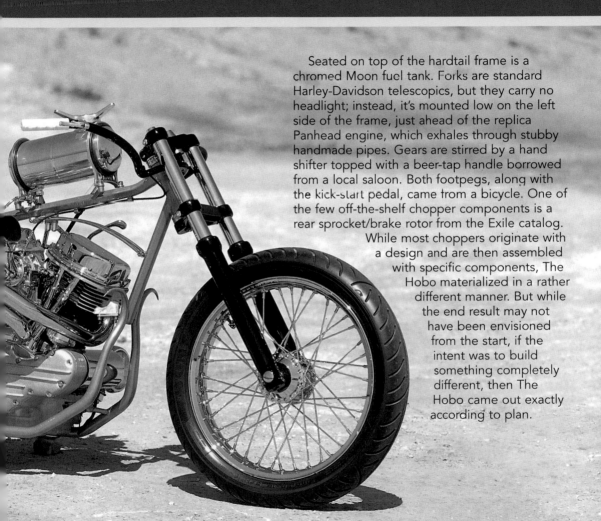

Seated on top of the hardtail frame is a chromed Moon fuel tank. Forks are standard Harley-Davidson telescopics, but they carry no headlight; instead, it's mounted low on the left side of the frame, just ahead of the replica Panhead engine, which exhales through stubby handmade pipes. Gears are stirred by a hand shifter topped with a beer-tap handle borrowed from a local saloon. Both footpegs, along with the kick-start pedal, came from a bicycle. One of the few off-the-shelf chopper components is a rear sprocket/brake rotor from the Exile catalog.

While most choppers originate with a design and are then assembled with specific components, The Hobo materialized in a rather different manner. But while the end result may not have been envisioned from the start, if the intent was to build something completely different, then The Hobo came out exactly according to plan.

The Hobo

Above: Handlebars were specially bent for the application; finger-activated throttle lever is from a jet ski, the handgrips from a Schwinn. *Top, left:* Shift knob lends a whole new meaning to the phrase "tap it into gear." *Right:* Replica "Panhead" engine, named for its pan-shaped valve covers, was built by RevTech and wears short, custom-made exhaust headers.

Note the unique taillight behind the transmission, and the headlight mounted low on the frame in front of the primary chain.

Oozn Evil

Arriving at the shop of Suicycles as a complete basket case, Oozn Evil gradually went together with catalog parts, pieces on hand, and a few custom-made components. After 12 long months, it was again ready to hit the streets.

The Harley-Davidson engine was treated to a number of aftermarket components, growing from its stock 74-cubic-inch displacement to 98 in the bargain. It also got a straight-pipe exhaust system custom-made by Suicycles. But the stock generator is used instead of a more modern alternator, the ignition remains the original point-and-condenser setup, and a kick starter still brings the engine to life.

Though the chassis incorporates a rear swingarm, solid struts replace the original shock absorbers, effectively making this a hardtail frame. A pair of Harley-Davidson Wide Glide front forks were extended 12 inches and hold a 21-inch spoke wheel with no brake. That leaves the braking chores to the large rear disc, which is attached to a 16-inch spoke wheel.

Like any bike that rolls out of Suicycle's shop, Oozn Evil is a study in low-tech componentry. But to many, that's only right and proper for an Old School design.

Oozn Evil

Above: Harley-Davidson's Shovelhead V-twin is an Old School staple. While some builders update them with modern electrics, this example retains its original generator, ignition system, and kick-starter. Note the solid strut that replaces the rear shock absorber, turning this into a hardtail frame.

Opposite page: Traditional "peanut" tank wears a blue-on-black flame paint scheme. Handlebars with perforated chrome grips sit on tall, chrome risers.

SPECIFICATIONS

Owner: Dan Hanson

Builder: Suicycles

Model: Oozn Evil

Frame: Harley-Davidson, 12 up, 6 out

Forks: Harley-Davidson, telescopic, 12 inches over

Rake: 38 degrees

Rear susp.: Swingarm w/solid struts

Front wheel: Spoke, 21-inch

Front brake: None

Rear wheel: Spoke, 16-inch

Rear tire: 150 mm

Rear brake: Disc

Engine: 98-cubic-inch Harley-Davidson

Exhaust: Suicycles

Trans.: Harley-Davidson, 4-speed

Paint by: MNK Customs

Dirty Love

year: 2002
builder: Suicycles
class: Old School

Suicycles is in the business of building high-performance, yet low-technology scoots. Very little in the way of flashy paint or highly polished alloys will be found on its machines. While some of the creations embody a bit more pizzazz, this one is pure performance in a plain black wrapper.

Though assembled from a combination of hardware, most major pieces hail from Harley-Davidson. The frame is from a 1949 model, the forks from a 1937. Power comes from a Harley Evo V-twin, which has been stroked from 80 to 89 cubic inches and massaged to produce more power.

The only form of "rear" suspension is found in the saddle, which provides three inches of travel courtesy of the chrome springs beneath. Finishing off this "no frills" machine is a matte black finish extending from the front forks to rear fender. A few bits of chrome dress the engine, but most noticeable is the shiny tool box mounted ahead of the rear axle. It's similar to those found on Harleys of old, which is exactly the look Suicycles strived to achieve.

Dirty Love

Straight handlebar wears no clutch lever, as the clutch is activated by a foot pedal (below).

Note the 8-ball knob on the stubby shift lever. A modern belt-drive primary substitutes for the original chain.

SPECIFICATIONS

Owner: Panhead Mike

Builder: Suicycles

Model: Dirty Love

Frame: Harley-Davidson

Forks: Harley-Davidson, springer

Rake: 35 degrees

Rear susp.: Hardtail

Front wheel: Spoke, 21-inch

Front brake: Drum

Rear wheel: Spoke, 16-inch

Rear tire: 140 mm

Rear brake: Drum

Engine: 89-cubic-inch Harley-Davidson

Exhaust: Suicycles

Trans.: Harley-Davidson, 4-speed, hand shift

Paint by: Suicycles

Above: *Machined rods make up the footpegs, brake "pedal," and brake arm. Old-time Bobbers were started with a kick lever, and this one is no different.* **Below:** *Rear-fender luggage rack is another throw-back to the past—and a handy one at that.*

Rigid

year: 2002
builder: Sound F/X Motorcycle Engineering
class: Old School

With years of chopper-building experience under its belt, Sound F/X Motorcycle Engineering wanted to try its hand at constructing a bike that wasn't dripping in gleaming lacquer and chrome. And thus began this venture into the Old School formula of design.

Sound F/X started with a CFL frame from Jesse James' West Coast Choppers, adding 8-inch-over forks from a Harley-Davidson Deuce mounted at a 42-degree rake. Red-rimmed Black Bike spoke wheels hold up each end, the front carrying a Harley disc brake, the rear fitted with a combination disc/sprocket from Exile.

An 80-cubic-inch Harley-Davidson V-twin is fitted with heads and internals from Headquarters. It inhales through an S&S carburetor with Maltese-cross air cleaner, while exhaust is handled by headers from Joker.

Completing the look is pinstriping done in the "Von Dutch" style over semimatte black paint. It all adds up to a fine first effort for a company new to the Old School of thought.

SPECIFICATIONS

Owner: Lou Mazzone

Builder: Sound F/X Motorcycle Engineering

Model: Rigid

Frame: West Coast Choppers, 4 up, 2 out

Forks: Harley-Davidson, telescopic, 8 inches over

Rake: 42 degrees

Rear susp.: Hardtail

Front wheel: Black Bike, 21-inch

Front brake: Disc

Rear wheel: Black Bike, 18-inch

Rear tire: 180 mm

Rear brake: Exile disc/sprocket

Engine: 80-cubic-inch Harley-Davidson

Exhaust: Joker

Trans.: Harley-Davidson, 5-speed

Paint by: Paint Spot

Above, right: Flying eyeball gracing the rear fender replicates artist Von Dutch's signature logo. He is famous for his pinstriping designs, the likes of which are also portrayed on this bike. **Right:** Maltese-cross air cleaner is emblazoned with "Sound FX" tumblin' dice graphics.

Suicide Jockey

year: 2004
builder: Ideal Ride
class: Old School

Like many Old School bikes, Suicide Jockey is a combination of old and new, though this configuration, built by Ideal Ride, incorporates some unusual pairings.

The original Harley-Davidson frame was replaced by a mildly stretched hardtail chassis from Paughco. Forks are largely the original Harley-Davidson components, but stretched eight inches and mounted at a more aggressive 40-degree rake. Eighty-spoke wheels used at both ends adhere to the traditional Old School formula, though disc brakes bring modern stopping power.

The 4-speed hand-shift transmission and some of the engine components are original from the 1955 Harley donor bike. But although the V-twin maintains its vintage Panhead look, modern high-performance components are fitted. The truncated exhaust pipes are the work of Ideal Ride.

A graceful, teardrop fuel tank sits behind "Z bar" handlebars mounted on chrome risers. The suspended solo saddle pivots at the front, acting on "mousetrap" springs at the rear. Basic black paint imparts a bad-boy demeanor to this striking mix of vintage and modern thought.

Suicide Jockey

Though incorporating many modern pieces, the V-twin wears its original "upside-down roasting pan" valve covers that prompted riders to nickname it the "Panhead." Note it also maintains its kick-starter.

SPECIFICATIONS

Owner: Joe Boris

Builder: Ideal Ride

Model: Suicide Jockey

Frame: Paughco, 2.5 up

Forks: Harley-Davidson, telescopic, 8 inches over

Rake: 40 degrees

Rear susp.: Hardtail

Front wheel: Spoke, 18-inch

Front brake: Disc

Rear wheel: Spoke, 18-inch

Rear tire: 180 mm

Rear brake: Disc

Engine: 80-cubic-inch Harley-Davidson

Exhaust: Ideal Ride

Trans.: Harley-Davidson, 4-speed, hand shift

Paint by: Paint Spot

Modern "open" belt-drive primary (engine to transmission) replaces the original chain that ran inside a cover. The covers often leaked oil, making this replacement a cleaner alternative.

Special Construction bikes are typically built largely from factory- or catalog-supplied components, but with several unique twists—and since an after-market frame is often among them, they usually aren't just stock bikes with added accessories. In some cases, bikes fall into this category simply because they didn't fit comfortably anywhere else. And for many people, a bike that's difficult to categorize makes it all the more appealing.

SPECIAL
CONSTRUCTION

DOUBLE TROUBLE

At first glance, Double Trouble might look like a mildly customized Harley-Davidson, as many of its pieces started out as stock Harley components. But closer inspection reveals that most of those parts have been modified and are attached to an aftermarket frame, putting the bike squarely into the Special Construction category.

The frame in question is a hardtail out of the Paughco (pronounced "Pa-ko") catalog. Large-diameter Harley FL forks were chosen for control and style, though they're stretched eight inches and mounted at a 40-degree rake for a more-aggressive profile.

With the exception of its Rev Tech carburetor and Samson exhaust system, the 80-cubic-inch Harley Evo V-twin remains true to its origins, with all internal components being stock. Also carried over is the Harley Fat Bob fuel tank, though the original top-mounted instrument panel has been replaced by a skunk pelt—which is what gave the bike its nickname of "Stinky." A ducktail rear fender and custom paint job complete a look that ensures Double Trouble is never mistaken for a production bike—at least, not by those in the know.

DOUBLE TROUBLE

Left: Hefty Harley-Davidson FL-style forks aren't commonly used on choppers, but look right at home on this beefy machine.

Right: Ducktail rear fender is similar to those used on some Harleys.

Fat Bob tank wears a skunk pelt in lieu of its usual instrument panel—a fair trade in the world of choppers.

SPECIFICATIONS

Owner: Tweety

Builder: Tweety/Ideal Ride

Model: Double Trouble

Frame: Paughco

Forks: Harley-Davidson, telescopic, 8 inches over

Rake: 40 degrees

Rear susp.: Hardtail

Front wheel: Spoke, 21-inch

Front tire: Dual disc

Front brake: Spoke, 16-inch

Rear wheel: 200 mm

Rear brake: Disc

Engine: 80-cubic-inch Harley-Davidson

Exhaust: Samson

Trans.: Harley-Davidson, 5-speed

Paint by: Paint Spot

Above: Hardtail frame holds classic spoke wheels. Slash-cut exhaust pipes add a custom touch.

PURPLE HAZE

year: 1996
builder: Michael Bailey
class: Special Construction

Though first purchased by Michael Bailey in 1974, it was more than 20 years before his 1955 Harley-Davidson would get the chopper treatment. Instead of hiring the work out, he took on the task himself—which resulted in a two-year build time.

A stretched Atlas hardtail frame was substituted for the original, providing a leaner look and more-radical profile. Girder forks replaced the heavy Hydra-Glide telescopics, and modern wheels and brakes were fitted at each end.

Displacement of the original Panhead V-twin remains at 74 cubic inches, but many parts have been replaced with modern, high-performance substitutes. The "Who's Who" list of internal hardware includes a Sifton cam, STD heads, S&S crank, and Wiseco pistons. A single SU carburetor tends the fuel mixture, which is lit by a Mallory ignition.

To complete his first project bike, Michael applied blue-to-red chameleon paint to every square inch of steel. A Harley-Davidson logo dresses the fuel tank, and a layer of chrome dresses the oil tank and forks.

It may have taken two decades for Michael to convert his old Harley into a stunning chopper, but judging from the outcome, it was worth the wait.

PURPLE HAZE

It may look like an old Panhead, and it may still displace 74 cubic inches, but the engine is loaded with high-performance hardware—including a chrome-plated SU carburetor and custom pipes bent by the builder.

Old-style girder forks add an unusual look to the front end, and an old-style Harley logo adds a vintage touch to the fuel tank.

SPECIFICATIONS

Owner: Michael Bailey

Builder: Michael Bailey

Model: Purple Haze

Frame: Atlas, 6 up, 2 out

Forks: Durfee girder, 15 inches over

Rake: 43 degrees

Rear susp.: Hardtail

Front wheel: Kennedy, 21-inch

Front brake: Performance Machine, dual disc

Rear wheel: Performance Machine, 16-inch

Rear tire: 160 mm

Rear brake: Performance Machine, disc

Engine: 74-cubic-inch Harley-Davidson

Exhaust: Michael Bailey

Trans.: Harley-Davidson, 4-speed

Paint by: Gordon Sipes

MODEL P

year: 2004
builder: Lifted Leg Customs
class: Special Construction

Not wanting to miss out on the chopper craze, Michael Agan decided to build his own. Operating under the name of Lifted Leg Customs, he began collecting the required components.

A Kraft Tech hardtail frame was chosen as the starting point, as it provided a classic chopper profile without going to extremes. A set of Harley-Davidson Wide Glide forks was added, along with spoke wheels that carried stock Harley disc brakes.

Power comes from an 80-cubic-inch Harley Evo V-twin that has been hopped up with an Andrews cam and S&S carburetor. Exhaust pipes are Sampson Sawed-Off Shorties.

A spring-mounted saddle adds a bit of comfort, and both it and the handgrips are done in a bright red that contrasts nicely with the matte-black finish. A rear white-wall tire brings another touch of retro to the ride, which took the novice builder just three months to complete.

Wide whitewall tire brings a hot-rod look, as does the red seat, which features rear-mounted springs for a touch of comfort.

Above: Red bicycle-type handgrips match the seat. *Below:* Classic "peanut" fuel tank is painted flat black.

SPECIFICATIONS

Owner:	Michael Agan
Builder:	Lifted Leg Customs
Model:	P
Frame:	Kraft Tech, 4 up, 2 out
Forks:	Harley-Davidson, telescopic
Rake:	34 degrees
Rear susp.:	Hardtail
Front wheel:	Spoke, 21-inch
Front brake:	Disc
Rear wheel:	Spoke, 18-inch
Rear tire:	150 mm
Rear brake:	Disc
Engine:	80-cubic-inch Harley-Davidson
Exhaust:	Sampson Sawed-Off Shorties
Trans.:	Harley-Davidson, 5-speed
Paint:	Michael Agan

ASTROZOMBIE

year: 2005
builder: Jason Hart / Chopsmiths
class: Special Construction

If you spend any time around Jason Hart of Chopsmiths, you soon realize the word "stock" is simply not part of his bike-building vocabulary. Any time he sets his sights on building another chopper, very few off-the-shelf components will be used—and most of those will be modified.

A frame from RC Components was the starting point for Astrozombie, but—not surprisingly—it was tweaked a bit for

this application. So were the Harley-Davidson Deuce forks. A Harley Shovelhead engine enlarged to 93 cubic inches provides plenty of motivational force.

The exotic contours of the rear fender, fuel tank, and side plates all began life as flat sheets of metal; Jason hand-formed, polished, and finished them with the help of his son, Devan.

Despite the wide variety of lights available in the aftermarket, Jason wanted to make his own. The headlight is fashioned out of a piston from a Cummins diesel engine, the taillight from an early Ford stoplamp. So it can rightfully be said that, from head to tail, the Astrozombie is truly a custom-built machine.

SPECIFICATIONS

Owner:	Mark Walls
Builder:	Jason Hart/Chopsmiths
Model:	Astrozombie
Frame:	RC Components, 2 down
Forks:	Harley-Davidson, telescopic, 5 inches over
Rake:	42 degrees
Rear susp.:	Hardtail
Front wheel:	RC Components, 21-inch
Front brake:	RC Components, disc
Rear wheel:	RC Components, 18-inch
Rear tire:	240 mm
Rear brake:	Exile disc/sprocket
Engine:	93-cubic-inch Harley-Davidson
Exhaust:	Chopsmiths
Trans.:	6-speed
Paint by:	Chopsmiths

Above: Headlight is made from the piston of a Cummins diesel engine; it's held in place by its connecting rod. Taillight was donated by an old Ford automobile.

Left and above: Graceful fuel tank was hand-formed from separate pieces of metal. Even the hand-tooled saddle is unique to this bike.

RIGIDITY

SPECIFICATIONS

Owner: Dave Dupor

Builder: DD Custom Cycles

Model: Rigidity

Frame: Pro-One, 6 up, 4 out

Forks: Pro-One, telescopic, 12 inches over

Rake: 38 degrees

Rear susp.: Hardtail

Front wheel: DD Custom Cycles, 21-inch

Front brake: Pro-One, disc

Rear wheel: DD Custom Cycles, 18-inch

Rear tire: 250 mm

Rear brake: Pro-One, disc

Engine: 96-cubic-inch S&S

Exhaust: Paul Yaffe

Trans.: 6-speed

Paint: Alcalde Customs

When you build eye-catching machines like Dave Dupor of DD Customs does, you're going to get some celebrity attention. After seeing several of his earlier creations, a player from the NFL contacted Dave about building a bike for an upcoming charity ride.

From the Pro-One catalog came a 6-up, 4-out hardtail frame, 12-inch-over telescopic forks, and front and rear disc brakes. Black anodized wheels add a subtle luster that complements the gloss black paint accented with silver metalflake flames outlined in red.

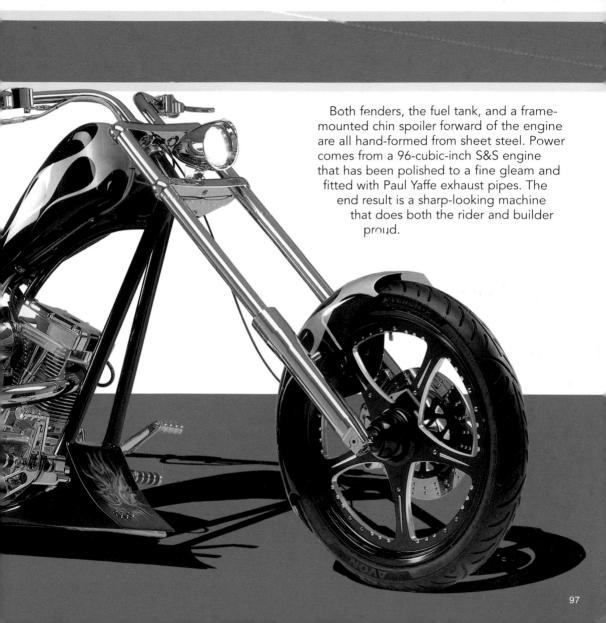

Both fenders, the fuel tank, and a frame-mounted chin spoiler forward of the engine are all hand-formed from sheet steel. Power comes from a 96-cubic-inch S&S engine that has been polished to a fine gleam and fitted with Paul Yaffe exhaust pipes. The end result is a sharp-looking machine that does both the rider and builder proud.

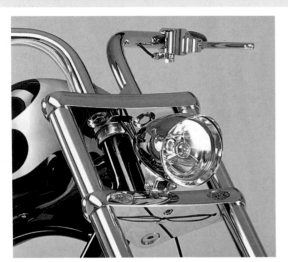

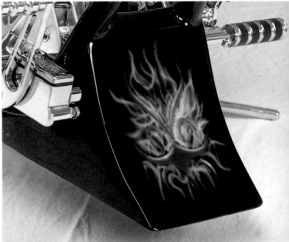

Above, left: Turn signals frenched into the lower triple tree give the bike legal lighting without the clutter of normal lenses. **Above and left:** Chin spoiler shares the sheet-metal's red-and-silver-on-black paint scheme.

REBEL

year: 1986
builder: X-Treme Cycle
class: Special Construction

Not all customs have to look like a Harley-Davidson, nor do they have to be big, expensive, and hard to ride.

John Lewis of X-Treme Cycle specializes in building big V-twin choppers, but when his wife Jeanne wanted a bike of her own, the situation called for something smaller. What seemed about the right size was a 250-cc Honda Rebel, but of course, it didn't offer the right look. Some customizing was in order, and this bike received a basketful.

For starters, the stock frame was modified with a longer swingarm, which was fixed in place with a solid link. That converted it to a hardtail frame with a lower profile and seat height. A short, sculpted rear fender replaced the original, and the standard fuel

tank was tossed in favor of a hand-formed "coffin" tank. A custom seat rides over a fat 16-inch rear wheel and tire that replaced the skinny stockers. Other custom touches include chopper-style head-light and taillight, high-flying fishtail mufflers, and silver metalflake flames over the black paint.

It just goes to show that customs can come in all shapes and sizes. The whole idea is to "have it your way," whatever that way might be.

REBEL

Straight handlebars with diamond-shaped mirrors and a lone instrument clean up the look from the driver's seat.

Left: Custom taillight is a modern chopper touch, while upswept fishtail mufflers mimic those from years past. Solid rods replace the rear shocks, lowering the bike's profile by giving it, in effect, a hardtail frame.

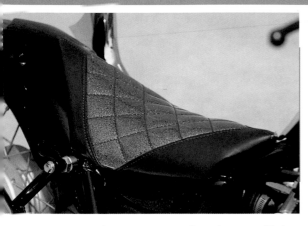

Seat insert matches the metalflake accents on the bike's sheetmetal.

SPECIFICATIONS

Owner: Jeanne Lewis
Builder: X-Treme Cycle
Model: Rebel
Frame: Honda
Forks: Honda, telescopic
Rake: 32 degrees
Rear susp.: Hardtail
Front wheel: Honda, 18-inch
Front tire: Honda, disc
Front brake: Honda, 16-inch
Rear wheel: 150 mm
Rear brake: Honda, drum
Engine: 15-cubic-inch Honda
Exhaust: X-Treme Cycle
Trans.: Honda, 5-speed
Paint by: Pro Body and Paint

Left: Coffin-shaped fuel tank is another throwback to yesteryear; barely visible are its glittery flames.

STUMP PULLER

year: 1999
builder: Ideal Ride
class: Special Construction

The desire for something less radical than a full-blown chopper brought Mike Young to Ideal Ride. What he wanted was a bike he could ride—with a passenger—on long trips with greater comfort than a traditional chopper could provide.

To this end, a Racing Innovations swingarm frame was used, which mounted the forks at a conservative—yet steeper than stock—38 degrees. RC Components 16-inch solid wheels polished to a mirror finish are used front and rear; each holds a disc brake with 4-piston calipers, also from RC Components.

Perhaps a bit less conservative is the power derived from the 96-cubic-inch S&S V-twin, which is far stronger than the stock engine, yet still smooth and reliable. It's backed up by a Rev Tech 5-speed transmission.

All painted surfaces are coated in Fire Red, with the sheetmetal, including a custom fuel tank from Beta, highlighted with silver flames. Big Harley-Davidson FL-style forks and oversized headlight add a massive look to the front end. It all adds up to a custom bike that doesn't discourage an all-day ride.

SPECIFICATIONS

Owner: Mike Young

Builder: Ideal Ride

Model: Stump Puller

Frame: Racing Innovations

Forks: Arlen Ness, telescopic

Rake: 38 degrees

Rear susp.: Triangulated swingarm

Front wheel: 18-inch

Front brake: Disc

Rear wheel: 18-inch

Rear tire: 180 mm

Rear brake: Disc

Engine: 96-cubic-inch S&S

Exhaust: Samson

Trans.: Rev Tech 5-speed

Paint by: Tim Alcalde

Beefy headlight and Harley FL-style forks lend a substantial look to the front end. So does the mirror-finished solid front wheel.

Seat can easily hold two riders in comfort.

Above: *Custom three-element taillight is barely visible against the Fire Red rear fender—until you hit the brakes.* **Left:** *S&S 96-cubic-inch engine is much stronger than a stock Harley V-twin, and with aftermarket air cleaner and exhaust pipes, is more striking as well.*

DUAL GLIDE

year: 1975
builder: Drago's Harley-Davidson Garage
class: Special Construction

As a longtime enthusiast and mechanic for all things Harley-Davidson, Drago Slimonia has seen a lot of trends come and go. When he decided to build a machine for himself, he wanted one that wouldn't look like anyone else's.

Starting with a 1975 Harley-Davidson FXE, he began to design and assemble this twin-suspension marvel. From the handlebars down, every inch of the front end has been handbuilt by Drago. The dual hydraulic fork legs are completely functional, and the multiangle bends in the handlebars are just as unusual.

Matching the forks is a quad shock setup for the rear swingarm, which necessitated a few changes to the otherwise-stock Harley frame. Also altered was the Harley's Shovelhead V-twin, which grew from 74 cubic inches to 101 and gained some hot-rodded parts in the bargain.

With its dual suspension and colorful graphics, Drago's chopper isn't likely to be confused with any other. Which means Drago got exactly what he wanted.

SPECIFICATIONS

Owner: Drago Slimonia

Builder: Drago's H-D Garage

Model: Dual Glide

Frame: Harley-Davidson/Drago

Forks: Drago, twin telescopic, 12 inches over

Rake: 32 degrees

Rear susp.: Swingarm

Front wheel: Harley-Davidson, 19-inch

Front brake: Disc

Rear wheel: Harley-Davidson, 16-inch

Rear tire: 150 mm

Rear brake: Disc

Engine: 101-cubic-inch Harley-Davidson

Exhaust: Cycle Shack

Trans.: Harley-Davidson 5-speed

Paint by: Ernie Levas

DUAL GLIDE

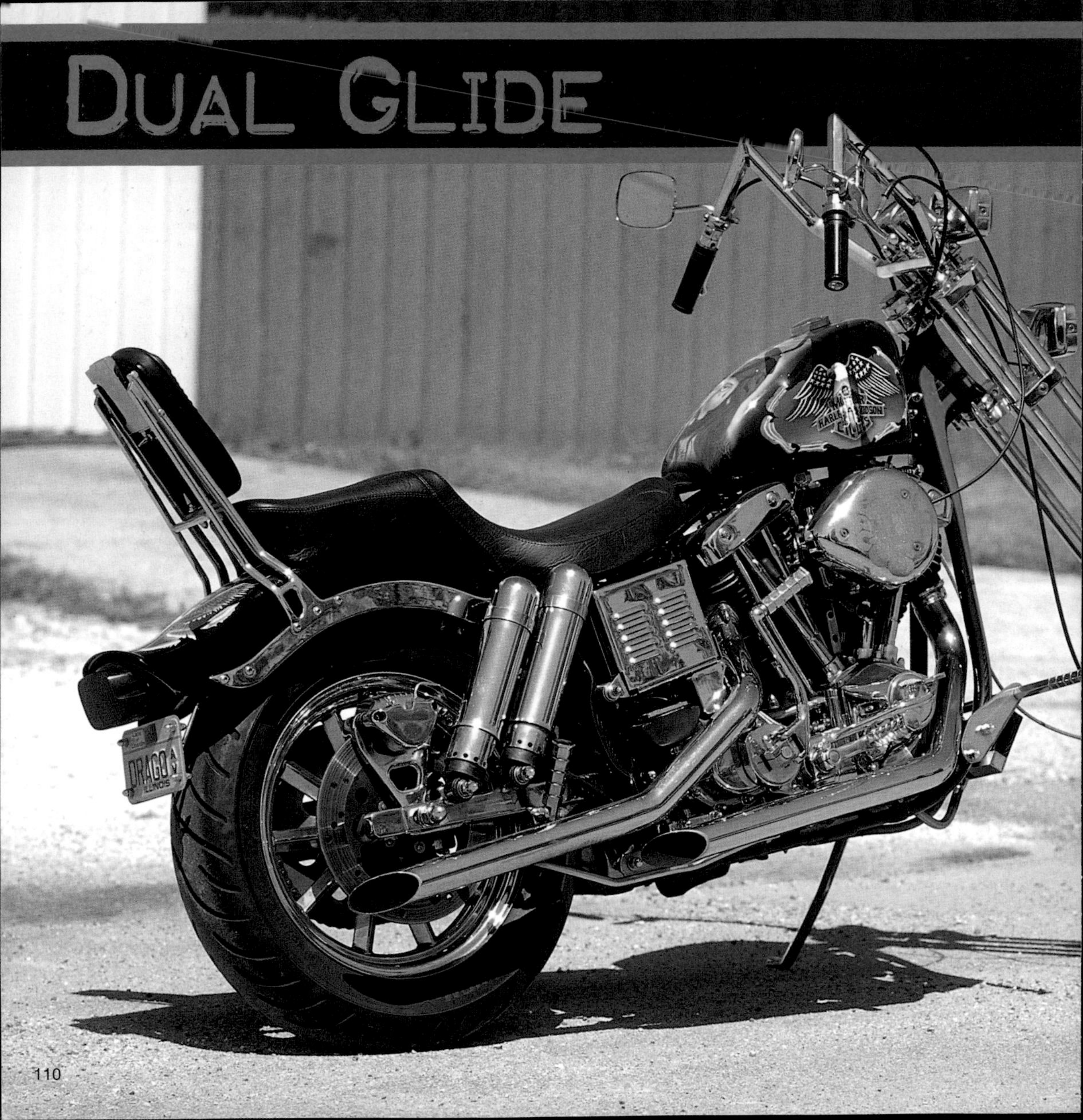

Opposite page: Most notable feature of the bike is the unique dual suspension. In front, twin forks run one atop the other; in back, two shocks run parallel on both sides of the bike. Note the stacked rectangular headlights, and the handlebars made from sharply angled hexagonal tubing. *Above:* Bike's design is duplicated in the tank graphics.

For many years, Mitchell, South Dakota, was known only for its Corn Palace. But now that Klock Werks has set up shop, it is also known as being the "Sportster Capital" of the United States.

Klock Werks primarily customizes Harley-Davidson Sportsters; a rare specialty, as most Harley customs start life as one of the company's larger Big Twins. For this exercise, Klock Werks modified a 1998 Sportster, smoothing the welds in the frame and molding curves into the tubing joints. A new swingarm allowed use of a wide 180-mm rear tire and a fender from the Jesse James catalog, which also supplied the front fender. The fuel tank was stretched, and revised triple trees gave the forks an extra five degrees of rake. All this resulted in a bike that looks longer and lower than a stock Sportster.

Further touches include a set of Performance Machine wheels, a digital gauge cluster, and "chopper style" head-light and taillight. Topping it all off is a metallic blue paint job highlighted with tribal flames hiding ghosted skulls.

Klock Werks' Sportsters are well-known in South Dakota, and are always a sight to behold. As an attraction in Mitchell, it appears the Corn Palace has some new competition.

Due to their taller, shorter stance, stock Sportsters seem a bit ungainly next to their rangier Big Twin brethren. Not so a Klock Werks Sportster, as a stretched tank and raked forks lean the look.

SPECIFICATIONS

Owner: Travis Boggs

Builder: Klock Werks

Model: Sportster

Frame: Harley-Davidson

Forks: APC, telescopic

Rake: 35 degrees

Rear susp.: Swingarm

Front wheel: Performance Machine, 21-inch

Front brake: Performance Machine, disc

Rear wheel: Performance Machine, 18-inch

Rear tire: 180 mm

Rear brake: Performance Machine, disc

Engine: 74-cubic-inch Harley-Davidson

Exhaust: Python

Trans.: Harley-Davidson, 5-speed

Paint by: Klock Werks

Custom touches abound, including chopper-style headlight and taillight, five-spoke wheels, and digital instrumentation. A dark blue base coat is set off by tribal flames engulfing a subtle skull motif.

By "factory," we don't mean Harley-Davidson. These choppers come from smaller enterprises typically producing less than 1000 bikes per year; by contrast, Harley builds upwards of 250,000 a year. The companies offer several models that can be individualized with different colors and paint schemes, providing many buyers the best of both worlds: a great-looking bike that stands out in a crowd, and instant delivery—with a warranty. Some buyers use them as merely a starting point, modifying them with their own special touches.

Factory & Factory- Modified

RETRO CHOPPER

Bourget's Bike Works (BBW) has been building extreme machines for many years, and one of its more radical designs is the Retro Chopper. By melding the apparent fuel tank and frame members into a single component, Bourget's achieves an unusually unified look.

It's an "apparent" fuel tank because the formed metal serves as little more than a broad canvas for applied graphics; in this case, the stars of a "Stars and Stripes" theme. Fuel and oil are carried within the frame tubes.

The 47-degree rake and 18-inch stretch of the springer forks makes for a radical front end. Equally notable is the

tail, which incorporates a labyrinth of tubing, but no suspension.

A 113-cubic-inch S&S engine sends power to a 280-series tire mounted on a BBW wheel that mimics the four-spoke "mag" style of the front rim. The rear axle rides in a machined tailpiece that also hosts the brake caliper.

Making this chopper stand out even more is its red, white, and blue paint scheme—as if this extreme machine needed to attract any more attention....

Below: *Long springer forks are held in intricately machined triple trees. Note equally elaborate mirrors.* **Right:** *What looks like a fuel tank is formed sheetmetal that has been blended into the frame tubes; gas and oil are held in the frame.*

Multitude of short tubes make up the rear of the frame. Holding the axle is a machined piece that also serves as a mount for the brake caliper.

SPECIFICATIONS

Owner: Ideal Ride

Builder: Bourget's Bike Works

Model: Retro Chopper

Frame: Bourget's Bike Works, 6 up, 6 out

Forks: Springer, 18 inches over

Rake: 47 degrees

Rear susp.: Hardtail

Front wheel: Bourget's Bike Works, 21-inch

Front brake: Bourget's Bike Works, disc

Rear wheel: Bourget's Bike Works, 18-inch

Rear tire: 280 mm

Rear brake: Bourget's Bike Works, disc

Engine: 113-cubic-inch S&S

Exhaust: Bourget's Bike Works

Trans.: 5-speed

Paint by: Bourget's Bike Works

LEGEND

year: 2004
builder: American IronHorse
class: Factory

AIH's choppers can he ordered with paintwork that rivals that of custom-built machines.

American IronHorse was founded by Bill Rucker and Tim Edmondson in 1995. Since then, the company has grown into one of the country's largest producers of "factory" choppers. Model offerings range from mild to wild, with the lineup growing every year.

The Legend is one of the more traditional models in AIH's line, but is still quite innovative. The frame, formed from large-diameter tubing, features a four-inch stretch and a triangulated-swingarm rear suspension. Forks are stretched six inches and mounted at a 38-degree rake. Wheels, brake rotors, and the drive pulley share the same design, and four-piston brake calipers are used on both wheels. A 21-inch tire is mounted up front, a 240-mm 18-incher in back. AIH produces its own saddles, and every Legend comes complete with an electronic digital instrument cluster.

A 107-cubic-inch S&S engine is the base powerplant, but larger 117- and 124-inch options can be ordered. The two-into-one exhaust by AIH extracts more power from the engine than traditional (for a chopper, anyway) two-into-two designs.

LEGEND

Wheel designs are carried over to the inner surfaces of the brake discs and drive pulley. Note the tapered, chromed fork sliders and machined foot controls—touches that define a custom.

SPECIFICATIONS

Owner: Ideal Ride

Builder: American IronHorse

Model: Legend

Frame: AIH, 4 up

Forks: AIH, telescopic, 6 inches over

Rake: 38 degrees

Rear susp.: Triangulated swingarm

Front wheel: AIH, 21-inch

Front brake: AIH, disc

Rear wheel: AIH, 18-inch

Rear tire: 240 mm

Rear brake: AIH disc

Engine: 107-cubic-inch S&S

Exhaust: AIH two-into-one

Trans.: 6-speed

Paint by: AIH

Below: AIH's two-into-one headers extract more power from the chrome-trimmed S&S engine.

Above: Handlebar risers and handgrips sport a custom appearance. A digital speedometer is standard, along with mirrors and turn signals; all are required in some states. The colored "eyebrow" in the half-moon speedometer housing is a bar-graph tachometer.

year: 2004
builder: Confederate
class: Factory

No, this is not your normal chopper. But then, it was never intended to be.

In an effort to build a bike unlike any other, Confederate combined high levels of technology with high performance to create the Hellcat 124. The company designed and built the frame, adding inverted Marzocchi forks, a Penske coil-over rear shock, and substantial brakes: twin 300-mm discs with 6-piston calipers in front, a 280-mm disc with twin-piston caliper in back. This impressive list of high-performance hardware is warranted because the 124-cubic-inch S&S Super Sidewinder Plus engine puts out an impressive 130 rear-wheel horsepower. The quest for speed is aided by bodywork crafted from carbon fiber, which not only saves weight, but with its matte finish and "weaved" appearance, lends a certain mystique as well.

Yes, a serious sporting demeanor makes the Hellcat unlike other choppers. But that was, of course, the intent all along.

SPECIFICATIONS

Owner:	Windwalkers Motorcycles of Naperville
Builder:	Confederate
Model:	Hellcat 124
Frame:	Confederate
Forks:	Marzocchi, inverted
Rake:	27 degrees
Rear susp.:	Swingarm
Front wheel:	Lightcon, 18-inch
Front brake:	Confederate, dual disc
Rear wheel:	Lightcon, 18-inch
Rear tire:	240 mm
Rear brake:	Confederate, disc
Engine:	124-cubic-inch S&S
Exhaust:	Confederate
Trans.:	Confederate 5-speed, right-side drive
Paint by:	Bodywork is natural carbon fiber

HELLCAT 124

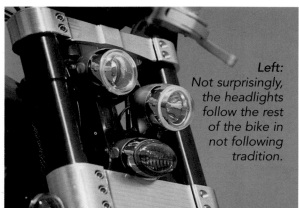

Left:
Not surprisingly, the headlights follow the rest of the bike in not following tradition.

Above, opposite page top: Carbon-fiber bodywork is usually found on high-end sportbikes, not choppers. But the Hellcat blends two distinctly different kinds of bikes into one decidedly unique machine.

Left: The body-work and behemoth brakes may say "sport-bike," but the ground-pounding 124-cubic-inch V-twin says "chopper." Note the curved swingarm, which doubles as the muffler housing. It's connected to the exhaust header with a flexible piece of piping.

SLAMMER

year: 2004
builder: America IronHorse
class: Factory

As the name implies, the Slammer from American IronHorse shuns the tall, raked appearance of many choppers for a low, stretched look. It is one of many bikes offered by the Texas-based company.

A rear swingarm smooths the bumps with help from an adjustable air-ride suspension, and a strutless rear fender results in a cleaner look. Up front, telescopic forks sit at a 42-degree rake (38-degree frame rake plus 4 degrees in the trees).

Details are similar to those of other American IronHorse rides. The drive pulley and brake rotors mimic the design of the wheels, which can be chosen from a host of different styles. The drivetrain consists of a 6-speed transmission and a 111-cubic-inch S&S engine exhaling through a 2-into-1 exhaust system. Turn signals and a digital speedometer (with bar-graph tachometer) conform to state registration requirements. And an extensive palette of paint colors and schemes ensure the long, low Slammer doesn't fade into the crowd.

Right: Manufacturer references are subtle: The IronHorse logo graces the clutch cover, and the company name is spelled out on the upper triple tree. *Below:* Wheel design carries over to the brake-disc hubs.

Available factory paint choices include this "rip and tear" diamond-plate scheme.

SPECIFICATIONS

Owner: Windwalkers Motorcycles of Naperville

Builder: American IronHorse

Model: Slammer

Frame: AIH hardtail, 2 out

Forks: AIH telescopic, 10 inches over

Rake: 42 degrees

Rear susp.: Swingarm with adjustable air ride suspension

Front wheel: AIH, 21-inch

Front brake: AIH, dual discs

Rear wheel: AIH, 18-inch

Rear tire: 240 mm

Rear brake: AIH disc

Engine: 111-cubic-inch S&S

Exhaust: AIH

Trans.: 6-speed

Paint by: AIH

TEXAS CHOPPER

Of all the bikes American IronHorse builds, the Texas Chopper displays the most extreme geometry and appearance. Lengthy chrome forks are mated with a stretched fuel tank that reaches all the way back to the seat. The choice of "real flame" paint only adds to the radical look.

Power for this example comes from a 117-cubic-inch S&S V-twin; it's the midsized engine offered for this model, the others displacing 111 and 124 cubic inches. All Texas Choppers come with a 6-speed gearbox regardless of powerplant.

In addition to a wide choice of colors and graphics, American IronHorse offers a selection of 12 different wheel styles. The Gladiator pattern was chosen for this model, and as with all AIH machines, the wheels, drive pulley, and brake rotors are cut in the same design. Extensive use of polished billet pieces makes this stand-out machine stand out even more.

SPECIFICATIONS

Owner: Windwalkers Motorcycles of Naperville

Builder: American IronHorse

Model: Texas Chopper

Frame: AIH hardtail, 8 up, 4 out

Forks: AIH telescopic, 10 inches over

Rake: 38 degrees

Rear susp.: Swingarm

Front wheel: AIH Gladiator, 21-inch

Front brake: AIH, dual discs

Rear wheel: AIH Gladiator, 18-inch

Rear tire: 240 mm

Rear brake: AIH, disc

Engine: 117-cubic-inch S&S

Exhaust: AIH

Trans.: 6-speed

Paint by: AIH

TEXAS CHOPPER

Left: Pattern of the Gladiator wheels—one of many styles offered—is reflected in the drive pulley and brake rotors.

Left: "Real flame" paint's soft edges make the fire look more...well...real. Eyebrow gauge panel just ahead of the forks holds a digital speedometer and bar-graph tachometer.

300 VM APPALOOSA

Having been in the business of building choppers since 1989, Surgical-Steeds has amassed a proven track record. So its latest offering, the classically designed, technologically advanced 300 VM Appaloosa, has a long history behind it.

Heavy-gauge tubing is used to form the chassis, including the 2-inch-diameter downtube, which is curved for style and strength. Surgical-Steeds' Monoglide chassis was introduced in 1996, utilizing an under-seat, fully adjustable spring/shock unit to control motions of the spade-shaped swingarm. The need for a separate oil tank has been eliminated by storing the required lubricant in the transmission case.

Buyers wanting to build it themselves can purchase the Surgical-Steeds chassis in kit form. The frame was designed to accept any Harley-Davidson V-twin, including the new Twin Cam 88. Those purchasing a complete machine can opt for a 111- or 124-cubic-inch S&S engine. Either way, buyers end up with a machine that not only has a long history behind it, but an equally long future ahead.

SPECIFICATIONS

Owner: Windwalkers Motorcycles of Naperville

Builder: Surgical-Steeds

Model: 300 VM Appaloosa

Frame: Surgical-Steeds, 8 up, 5 out

Forks: Ceriani, inverted

Rake: 40 degrees

Rear susp.: Swingarm

Front wheel: Surgical-Steeds, 21-inch

Front brake: Disc

Rear wheel: Surgical-Steeds, 18-inch

Rear tire: 300 mm

Rear brake: Disc

Engine: 111-cubic-inch S&S

Exhaust: Surgical-Steeds

Trans.: Baker 6-speed, right-side drive

Paint by: Surgical-Steeds

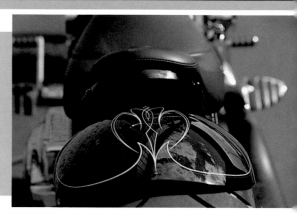

Rear wheel is accented with the same red-and-white striping that graces the frame and sheetmetal. Note the spade-shaped swingarm.

Above: The under-seat spring/shock for the rear suspension is fully adjustable for comfort and chrome-plated for pizzazz.
Left: This example is fitted with a 111-cubic-inch S&S engine with special air cleaner and 2-into-1 exhaust, but for those "do-it yourselfers" starting with a chassis kit, the frame is designed to hold any Harley-Davidson V-twin.

year: 2004
builder: Wicked Women Choppers
class: Factory

Women tend to be smaller in stature than men, and those wanting to ride their own chopper often have trouble finding one that will fit their frames. Christine Vaughn was one of these women, and she decided to do something about it. Her company, Wicked Women Choppers, is devoted to building machines designed for the female rider.

The 2004 Shady Lady is built around a frame that keeps both the seat height and center of gravity closer to the ground. Chassis geometry is pure chopper, but not so extreme as to cause difficulties reaching the controls, which is also the intent of handlebars configured with a smaller rider in mind.

While built for a woman, the Shady Lady is strong enough for a man. The polished 96-cubic-inch S&S engine provides plenty of motivation, regardless of the rider's size.

Choppers are all about individuality and having a bike that's tailor-made for you—no matter what size you wear. And like the clients they serve, Wicked Women Choppers proves once again that good things often come in smaller packages.

SHADY LADY

Pink-heart flames isn't the only paint scheme offered by Wicked Women Choppers, but it is perhaps the most ladylike. Note the dropped seat, pull-back handlebars, and close-in pedals that make the bike better suited to shorter riders.

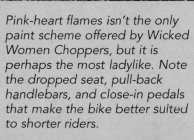

SPECIFICATIONS

Owner: Wicked Women Choppers

Builder: Wicked Women Choppers

Model: Shady Lady

Frame: Wicked Women Choppers, 4 up, 2 out

Forks: RC Components, telescopic, 6 inches over

Rake: 38 degrees

Rear susp.: Progressive, swingarm

Front wheel: RC Components, 21-inch

Front brake: RC Components, disc

Rear wheel: RC Components, 18-inch

Rear tire: 250 mm

Rear brake: RC Components, disc/pulley

Engine: 96-cubic-inch S&S

Exhaust: Wicked Bros.

Trans.: Primo/Rivera 6-speed, right-side drive

Paint by: Wicked Women Choppers

American IronHorse sells a number of different motorcycles in a variety of designs through more than 100 dealers in the United States. Each bike can be customized with a selection of wheels and colors.

The basis for the LSC is a hardtail frame with 4-inch stretch, 8-inch rise, and 38-degree rake in the neck. Triple trees add another four degrees, for a total of 42 degrees of fork rake. Forks are 12-inch-over telescopics, and combine with the tall frame for an extreme stance. A 124-cubic-inch S&S engine is fitted to this example, but 107- and 113-cubic-inch versions are also available. The 6-speed transmission has right-side belt drive.

The wheels shown are AIH's Lonestars; their design is echoed in the brake rotors and drive pulley. Two features of the LSC not found on many choppers are the strutless rear fender, which provides a cleaner appearance, and dual front brakes for better stopping power.

It may be a "factory" bike, but the LSC boasts plenty of custom touches, such as the sculpted front and rear fenders. Arched chrome bars hold the strutless rear fender and turn signals, the latter required of factory bikes in many states.

Above: Slender oil tank allows a lower seat height. *Below:* Dual front disc brakes are a welcome sight on a chopper with 124 cubic inches of power. Note the duplication of the wheel pattern in the disc hub.

SPECIFICATIONS

Owner:	Ideal Ride
Builder:	American IronHorse
Model:	LSC
Frame:	AIH, 8 up, 4 out
Forks:	AIH telescopic, 12 inches over
Rake:	42 degrees
Rear susp.:	Hardtail
Front wheel:	AIH Lonestar, 21-inch
Front brake:	AIH dual discs
Rear wheel:	AIH Lonestar, 18-inch
Rear tire:	280 mm
Rear brake:	AIH disc
Engine:	124-cubic-inch S&S
Exhaust:	AIH
Trans.:	6-speed, right-side drive
Paint by:	AIH

DropSeat 280

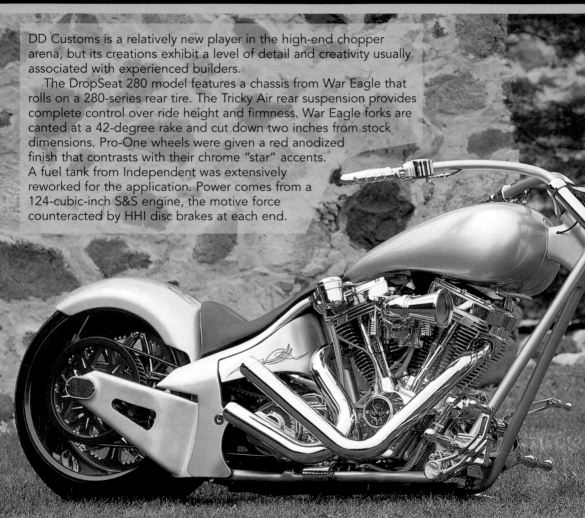

DD Customs is a relatively new player in the high-end chopper arena, but its creations exhibit a level of detail and creativity usually associated with experienced builders.

The DropSeat 280 model features a chassis from War Eagle that rolls on a 280-series rear tire. The Tricky Air rear suspension provides complete control over ride height and firmness. War Eagle forks are canted at a 42-degree rake and cut down two inches from stock dimensions. Pro-One wheels were given a red anodized finish that contrasts with their chrome "star" accents. A fuel tank from Independent was extensively reworked for the application. Power comes from a 124-cubic-inch S&S engine, the motive force counteracted by HHI disc brakes at each end.

Subtle Silver Candy paint seems to glow in the light, and is accented with Von Dutch-style striping. It all results in an exceptional bike with a unique look that does the newcomers at DD Customs proud.

SPECIFICATIONS

Owner: Dave Dupor

Builder: DD Customs

Model: DropSeat 280

Frame: War Eagle 280

Forks: War Eagle, telescopic, 2 inches under

Rake: 42 degrees

Rear susp.: Swingarm w/adjustable air suspension

Front wheel: Pro-One, 21-inch

Front brake: HHI, disc

Rear wheel: Pro-One, 18-inch

Rear tire: 280 mm

Rear brake: HHI, disc

Engine: 124-cubic-inch S&S

Exhaust: Sampson Zoomies

Trans.: 5-speed, right-side drive

Paint by: MNK Custom Works

DROPSEAT 280

Glowing Silver Candy paint is set off by the type of free-form pinstriping popularized by artist Von Dutch in the 1960s. Red anodized wheels give off a radiance of their own.

year: 1999
builder: Crown Custom Cycle Fabrications
class: Factory-Modified

Crown Custom Cycle Fabrication (CCCF) has forged a reputation for high performance machinery, but can also build bikes with as much "show" as "go." And Creep Show is one of them.

Added to a Bourget's Bike Works frame was a set of 6-inch-over Progressive telescopic forks set at a 42-degree rake. Weld Wheels carrying JB disc brakes hold up both ends. Providing power is a 113-cubic-inch engine from TP Engineering. Nearly every junction in the hardtail frame has been molded smooth, including those on the fabricated brace for the rear fender. Elaborate graphics atop the fuel tank depict a wizard fending off invading demons, but perhaps the most striking visual element is the "chameleon" paint, which flips from purple to green depending on the angle of view. Static display on a page fails to do the paint job justice, but what does are the numerous trophies picked up at major cycle events—proving this bike really is for "show" as much as for "go."

CREEP SHOW

Fuel tank shows off the "Wizard and Demons" theme, along with the "chameleon" paint that flips from purple to green, depending on viewing angle.

Rear fender brace is molded into the frame, as are nearly all of the tubing joints. Oil tank "eyes" passersby.

SPECIFICATIONS

Owner: Walter Anderson

Builder: Crown Custom Cycle Fabrications (CCCF)

Model: Creep Show

Frame: Bourget's Bike Works

Forks: Progressive, telescopic, 12 inches over

Rake: 40 degrees

Rear susp.: Hardtail

Front wheel: Weld, 21-inch

Front brake: JB, Disc

Rear wheel: Weld, 18-inch

Rear tire: 300 mm

Rear brake: JB, Disc

Engine: 113-cubic-inch TP Engineering

Exhaust: Sampson Street Sweeper

Trans.: 5-speed

Paint by: Bud Dennis and Jim Brando

CHOPPER

There are a number of factory-built choppers on the market today, and their accessibility and price prove attractive to many buyers. But not everyone is content to leave well enough alone.

One advantage of a factory-built chopper is the predetermined frame geometry and suspension setup; there's less worry that a chosen fork stretch and rake will handle poorly or won't work well with the desired frame. Factory models have usually been engineered to deliver optimum performance as they roll off the line.

That doesn't mean, however, that buyers must leave them that way. For many, factory-built choppers are just a blank canvas to be painted by their imagination.

Which is exactly how this creation came about. Independence Choppers offers a varied lineup, the Chopper model being the most radical. From there, the front fender was removed to add an Old School flavor, and the black paint was augmented with custom pinstriping. Then a set of Yaffe X-Pipes and other distinctive touches were added, all ensuring another just like it won't be seen around the next corner.

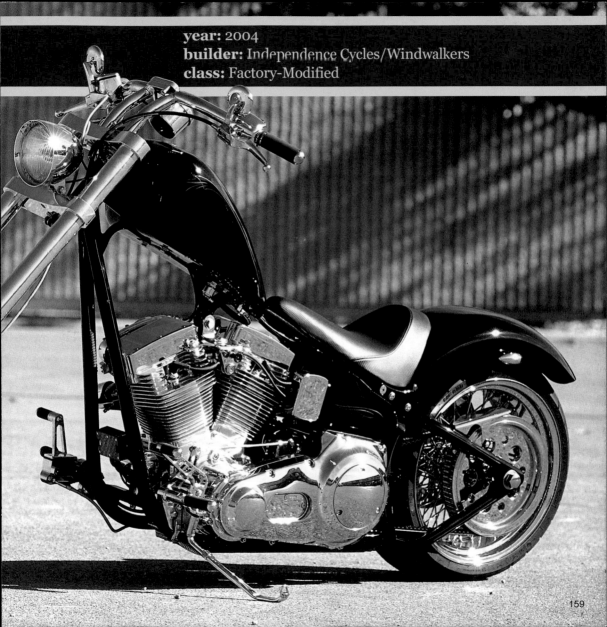

year: 2004
builder: Independence Cycles/Windwalkers
class: Factory-Modified

Substituting a different air cleaner and exhaust system help individualize a factory-built bike, as does adding custom pinstriping.

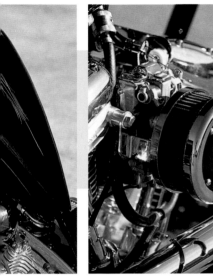

SPECIFICATIONS

Owner: Sam Herron

Builder: Independence Choppers/
Windwalkers Motorcycles
of Naperville

Model: Chopper

Frame: Independence Choppers,
8 up, 4 out

Forks: Independence Choppers,
inverted, 10 inches over

Rake: 41 degrees

Rear susp.: Triangulated swingarm

Front wheel: Independence Choppers,
21-inch

Front brake: Disc

Rear wheel: Independence Choppers,
18-inch

Rear tire: 240 mm

Rear brake: Disc

Engine: 110-cubic-inch Rev Tech

Exhaust: Yaffe X-Pipes

Trans.: Rev Tech, 6-speed

Paint: Independence Choppers/
Striping by Liza

HigH RolleR

Owner: Kevin Murphy

Builder: American Performance Cycles/ Windwalkers

Model: High Roller

Frame: APC, 7 up, 4 out

Forks: APC, inverted, 10 inches over

Rake: 38 degrees

Rear susp.: Swingarm

Front wheel: APC, 21-inch

Front brake: Hawg Halter, disc

Rear wheel: APC, 18-inch

Rear tire: 280 mm

Rear brake: Hawg Halter, disc

Engine: 124-cubic-inch S&S

Exhaust: APC

Trans.: 6-speed, right-side drive

Paint by: Brian Evans

American Performance Cycles produces a variety of models, and the High Roller 280 RHD is its top-of-the-line machine. Nevertheless, some buyers prefer to take it a step or two beyond.

In addition to his passion for choppers, owner Kevin Murphy has an equally avid love for guitars. Blending the two interests produced the creation shown here.

The starting point was an APC frame with four-inch stretch, seven-inch rise, and Soft-Ride rear suspension. Ten-inch-over inverted forks are raked at 38 degrees. A 124-cubic-inch S&S engine combines with a 6-speed transmission to add "go" to the "show."

Every piece of sheetmetal is painted in a guitar motif, but there are several other custom touches as well. The primary cover is an artful display of machine work, as is the kickstand. Together, they help make this bike a very high roller indeed.

Details are what set modified factory bikes apart from their "mass-produced" brethren; note the engraving on the headlight bucket and kickstand. But the paint job is what really sets a machine apart, and this guitar theme—based on the drawings of a twelfth-century Japanese monk—does the trick. The spear-shaped swingarm is another nice touch.

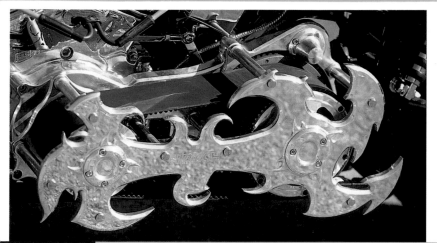

It's machine work like this primary cover that really adds to the uniqueness—and cost—of a bike.

Scallops cut into the ends of the exhaust pipes give them a custom look.

Today, numerous companies offer prebuilt "factory" choppers for sale to the public. But back in 2002 when this machine was built, that wasn't the case. There were, however, catalogs offering parts that could be purchased on an *á la carte* basis, and then assembled into a chopper. And this is a prime example of such a machine.

Starting with a Kraftech hardtail frame, Scooter Shooterz of Indiana added 12-inch-over Pro-Tech telescopic forks, a fuel tank from Independent, and a Rev Tech powertrain. Sixty-spoke wheels from DNA, a custom seat designed by Scooter Shooterz, and an exhaust system from L.A. Choppers helped make it ridable. Scooter Shooterz then finished it off with tangerine paint hosting graffiti graphics, and *voilá*—another chopper was born.

Right: *Scooter Shooterz designed the seat, then had it upholstered. There's probably not another like it.*

Left: *Engine is a standard Rev Tech item, but a Flowmaster intake and L.A. Choppers exhaust—along with lots of chrome plating—help set it off.*

Above: *Catalogs may offer some nice-looking parts, but fine paintwork still stands out.*

SPECIFICATIONS

Owner: Roger Lange

Builder: Scooter Shooterz

Model: Catalog Bike

Frame: Kraftech, 8 up

Forks: Pro One telescopic, 12 inches over

Rake: 43 degrees

Rear susp.: Hardtail

Front wheel: DNA Spoke, 21-inch

Front brake: Disc

Rear wheel: DNA Spoke, 18-inch

Rear tire: 250 mm

Rear brake: Disc

Engine: 100-cubic-inch Rev Tech

Exhaust: L.A. Choppers

Trans.: Rev Tech, 6-speed

Paint by: Scooter Shooterz

Left: *Classic wire-spoke wheels may not look as fancy as machined wheels, but many riders feel they're what motorcycles are supposed to have— whether stock or custom.*

As the name implies, Radical choppers are over-the-edge creations incorporating lots of custom machine work and lavish paint jobs. Their frames and sheetmetal are rarely straight from a factory or catalog; they're usually modified or handmade and thus unique. The "manufacturers" can be companies making a few bikes a year for well-heeled buyers, or backyard builders toiling on their own creations. But the bottom line is that the best of these stretch the imagination—and sometimes, the limits of reason.

Radical

Suicide Softail

For Pain Erickson, not just any chopper would do. Thinking others might feel the same, he decided to build a series of bikes that met his own exacting standards.

One was this Candy Red Suicide Softail. As the name implies, it features a uniquely styled rear swingarm with adjustable air-spring suspension mounted behind the engine. And what an engine it is: 145 cubic inches of V-twin power, with custom-bent exhaust pipes wrapped in heat-shielding tape. A 6-speed Baker transmission with hand shifter feeds the ponies to a combination sprocket/rear brake affixed to a solid, chromed rear wheel.

Perhaps most distinctive, however, is the bodywork, all performed by Erickson himself. The frame was a joint effort between Thee Darkside of Daytona and Killer Choppers. Springer forks run at a steep rake of 68 degrees (most choppers are at 38-55 degrees), making for a huge turning radius. But then, it's doubtful Erickson ever intended this unique creation as an around-town grocery-getter.

Driver's-eye view reveals sculpted fuel tank topped by an extended fuel neck with spired cap.

Suicide Softail

SPECIFICATIONS

Owner: Pain Erickson

Builder: Thee Darkside of Daytona

Model: Suicide Softail

Frame: Thee Darkside of Daytona/ Killer Choppers, 4 out

Forks: Springer

Rake: 68 degrees

Rear susp.: Swingarm w/air- adjustable suspension

Front wheel: West Coast Choppers, 21-inch

Front brake: Performance Machine, disc

Rear wheel: Chrome Smoothies, 18-inch

Rear tire: 300 mm

Rear brake: Exile, disc/sprocket

Engine: 145-cubic-inch Ultima

Exhaust: Thee Darkside of Daytona

Trans.: Baker 6-speed, hand shift, right-side drive

Paint by: Got 2B Kustom

Opposite page, top: Transmission has a hand shifter rather than the more common foot shift. The shift knob doesn't appear to be contoured for comfort. *Left:* Lines running to the oil tank betray its camouflaged location below the frame neck. Most of the frame is encased in sculpted sheetmetal.

Right and opposite page, bottom: Rear sprocket by Exile is essentially a brake disc with teeth cut into its circumference. Incorporating two functions into one piece allows the left side of the wheel to run "naked," with nothing to obscure its dazzling chrome finish.

Bad Moon

year: 2003
builder: Kenny Rollins/ Chopper Shop, Inc.
class: Radical

Not only is the owner of this bizarre machine responsible for its design, he's also responsible for its creation.

Kenny Rollins built Bad Moon around a hardtail chassis from Killer Choppers, setting a springer fork from the Paughco catalog at a 49-degree rake. The 40-spoke front wheel has a single disc brake, and the Rader mag-style rear wheel is equipped with a combination brake disc/sprocket from Exile.

In between sits an 88-cubic-inch Rev Tech V-twin that combines the look of a vintage Harley-Davidson Panhead engine with the advantages of modern technology. The snakey exhaust system was custom-made by Rollins. A 5-speed Rev Tech transmission gets both hand- and foot-operated shifters.

Perhaps the most obvious design feature is the oversized Moon fuel tank. Coated in chrome, it is mounted directly to the upper frame tube. Other custom touches include a chromed, oval oil tank below the sprung saddle, and a tall, warped sissy bar. It all combines to create a very unusual machine, which is exactly what the owner wanted—and built.

Moon fuel tanks were popular on hot rods and dragsters of the '50s and '60s. A mere accessory on those vehicles, it takes center stage here. The tall Hurst shift lever beside it is another automotive icon of the 1960s.

Beneath the hot-rod-style pleated seat resides an oval oil tank with diamond-plate end caps.

Bad Moon

SPECIFICATIONS

Owner: Kenny Rollins

Builder: Kenny Rollins/ Chopper Shop, Inc.

Model: Bad Moon

Frame: Killer Choppers, 6 up, 3 out

Forks: Paughco, springer, 9 inches over

Rake: 49 degrees

Rear susp.: Hardtail

Front wheel: Spoke, 21-inch

Front brake: Disc

Rear wheel: Rader, 15-inch

Rear tire: 230 mm

Rear brake: Exile, disc/sprocket

Engine: 88-cubic-inch Rev Tech

Exhaust: Kenny Rollins

Trans.: Rev Tech 5-speed, hand and foot shift

Paint by: Russ

When was the last time you saw a chopper with whitewalls? Probably never. But both that and the mag-style rear wheel are reminiscent of old hot rods, and blend perfectly with the bike's 1960s motif.

Trop Chop

year: 2005
builder: Midwest Choppers
class: Radical

Chip Miyler of Midwest Choppers has earned a reputation for highly detailed, well-built choppers, and the Trop Chop is yet another testament to his many talents.

A stretched Midwest Choppers frame positions the neck two inches

up and five inches out, setting the extended American Suspension forks at a 48-degree rake. A rear swingarm with suspension by Progressive adds some comfort to the style.

Not willing to build an all-show, no-go chopper, Chip employed a 124-cubic-inch S&S engine for motivation. Matching Xtreme Machine rims host HHI disc brakes, and in back, a 280-mm tire.

But the real artistry of Trop Chop lies in the flowing bodywork and eye-catching paint scheme. Every inch of sheetmetal is of Chip's own creation, and the tropical scenes by Jeremy Imming detail underwater life in amazing imagery employing nearly every color of the spectrum. It all flows together to help cement Midwest Choppers' reputation as one of the country's premier builders.

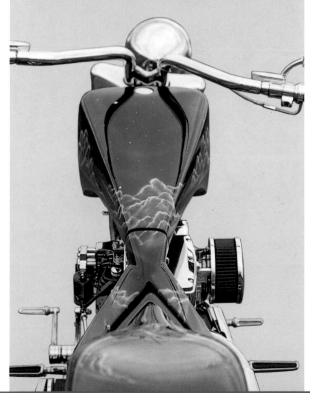

Trop Chop

A showcase of underwater imagery, Trop Chop hosts an eyeful of artistic brushwork. Not even the frame escaped the painter's touch.

SPECIFICATIONS

Owner: Chip Miyler

Builder: Midwest Choppers

Model: Trop Chop

Frame: Midwest Choppers,
2 up, 5 out

Forks: American Suspension,
inverted, 6 inches over

Rake: 48 degrees

Rear susp.: Progressive swingarm

Front wheel: Xtreme Machine,
21-inch

Front brake: HHI, disc

Rear wheel: Xtreme Machine,
18-inch

Rear tire: 280 mm

Rear brake: HHI, inboard
disc/pulley

Engine: 124-cubic-inch S&S

Exhaust: Martin Bros.

Trans.: Baker 6-speed,
right-side drive

Paint by: Jeremy Imming

Johnny Walker

year: 2004
builder: Top Shelf Customs
class: Radical

Todd Silicato had been involved in building high-end custom motorcycles for many years before deciding to create one of his own. Johnny Walker is the result, and it bristles with imagination and one-off components.

Most distinctive is the paintwork. Beige and white blend together on the sheetmetal, while wheels are finished in brown—an unusual color combination in the chopper world. But other elements are unusual as well, including the tooled leather seat, custom-bent exhaust, and lattice grillwork gracing the frame. The creased fuel tank is another unique piece, and it all combines to set Johnny Walker apart from the chopper crowd.

SPECIFICATIONS

Owner: Top Shelf Customs

Builder: Top Shelf Customs

Model: Johnny Walker

Frame: Independent Cycle Hard Life, 7 out

Forks: Jesse Rooke, girder

Rake: 40 degrees

Rear susp.: Hardtail

Front wheel: DNA Spokes, 21-inch

Front brake: none

Rear wheel: DNA Spokes, 18-inch

Rear tire: 300 mm

Rear Brake: Performance Machine, disc

Engine: 93-cubic-inch S&S with STD heads

Exhaust: Top Shelf Customs

Trans.: Baker 6-speed, right-side drive

Paint by: Color Zone

Exhaust pipes run on both sides of the bike—the right-side pipe making a loop behind the cylinder—and exit through lattice grilles set ahead of the rear axle.

Johnny Walker

Edgy fuel tank features a center spine topped with a "spinner" fuel cap.

Solid forks pivot at the base of the frame neck, compressing a spring mounted to the top of the neck. A similar design was used on bicycles of the '50s and '60s. **Below:** More hammock than saddle, the leather sling that passes as a seat is suspended between three posts.

Spoon

year: 2005
builder: Precious Metal Customs
class: Radical

Precious Metal Customs, formed in 1998, builds only radical machines, with most pieces being custom-made. For instance, whereas most manufacturers buy frames and sheetmetal off the shelf, PMC creates its own.

The Spoon rides a hardtail chassis carrying a 100-cubic-inch Harley-Davidson engine fitted with Rev Tech internal hardware. Among the bike's unusual features is a rearview camera and video screen that substitute for rearview mirrors—eliminating their often tacked-on look—while allowing the rider a clear view of what he's leaving behind.

Internal machining on the rear sprocket matches the design of the rear wheel. Red chain and axle cover put a colorful finishing touch on pieces that normally detract from the overall look.

Wicked Bros. exhaust pipes join in an unusual side-by-side design. A spire matching those used on footpegs and control pedals tops the air cleaner. Image from rearview camera is displayed on a video screen frenched into the top of the fuel tank.

Spoon

SPECIFICATIONS

Owner: Russ Austin

Builder: Precious Metal Customs

Model: Spoon

Frame: PMC, 5 up, 6 out

Forks: Mean Street, inverted 20 inches over

Rake: 50 degrees

Rear susp.: Hardtail

Front wheel: Xtreme Machine, 21-inch

Front brake: Hawg Halter, disc

Rear wheel: Xtreme Machine, 18-inch

Rear tire: 300 mm

Rear brake: Hawg Halter, disc

Engine: 100-cubic-inch Harley-Davidson

Exhaust: Wicked Bros.

Trans.: Baker 6-speed

Paint by: Flashback

Machined accents—many quite elaborate—dress the cylinders, primary-drive cover, and frame downtube. Spire-

topped footpegs and control
pedals follow a theme carried
throughout the bike.

Aggression

year: 2005
builder: Midwest Choppers
class: Radical

Aggression got off to a rocky start. Begun as a customer order that fell through, Chip Miyler at Midwest Customs decided to complete the project on his own.

A swingarm frame with rear suspension by Progressive mounts 8-inches-over inverted forks at a 51-degree rake. Extreme Machine wheels at both ends feature fine detailing. In front, the brake rotor matches the wheel design; in back, the pulley—which overlays the brake rotor—does the same.

Power comes from a 124-cubic-inch S&S engine polished to a show finish. Air enters through a Midwest Choppers air cleaner, exiting via a Martin Bros. exhaust system.

Elaborate sheetmetal work features a silver spine running from front fender to rear, bisecting the deep purple paint. An aggressive scoop is formed into the base of the frame's downtube, while both fenders wrap deeply around the tires.

As it turned out, six months of toil were required to complete the build, but a Best Radical Custom trophy at a show in Indianapolis made it all worthwhile. Aggression may have started on a low note, but certainly finished on a high one.

Aggression

Central spine appears on the frame, fenders, fuel tank, and even the seat. Air-cleaner cover has a matching ridge. Note serrated edges on the engine's cooling fins,

a rare custom touch. Also unusual are the small lights frenched into the rear section of the swingarm.

SPECIFICATIONS

Owner: Chip Miyler

Builder: Chip Miyler/
Midwest Choppers

Model: Aggression

Frame: Midwest Choppers,
4 up, 4 out

Forks: American Suspension,
inverted, 8 inches over

Rake: 51 degrees

Rear susp.: Progressive swingarm

Front wheel: Xtreme Machine,
21-inch

Front brake: HHI, disc

Rear wheel: Xtreme Machine, 18-inch

Rear tire: 280 mm

Rear brake: HHI, inboard disc/pulley

Engine: 124-cubic-inch S&S

Exhaust: Martin Bros.

Trans.: Accessories Unlimited
6-speed, right-side drive

Paint by: TT Customs

Low Blow

year: 2003
builder: Thee Darkside of Daytona
class: Radical

Nearly anyone with the right amount of know-how can assemble a nice-looking chopper. But to build a bike of this complexity, do nearly all the work in-house, and complete the job in just a month takes a shop like Thee Darkside of Daytona.

What separates Low Blow from most other choppers can be summed up in one word: horsepower. Gobs of it. More than any sane person would ever need—or use. Beneath the skull-ringed fuel tank sits a 124-cubic-inch V-twin pressure fed by a roots-type supercharger. And if for some unfathomable reason that's not enough, extra boost is just a squirt of nitrous oxide away. All that power is transferred through a 5-speed gearbox with hand shifter. Slowing the bike down is the duty of Performance Machine disc brakes at both ends.

Interesting decorative touches are another trademark of Thee Darkside of Daytona machines. The hardtail frame features a distinctly styled rear section, while a spined

backbone serves—worthlessly—as a rear fender. Forks ride at a radical 65-degree rake, which aids straightline stability when the horses stampede.

To think this all came together in a month's time is hard to imagine. But speedy work is Thee Darkside of Daytona's specialty—in more ways than one.

SPECIFICATIONS

Owner: Pain Erickson

Builder: Thee Darkside of Daytona

Model: Low Blow

Frame: Thee Darkside of Daytona/ Killer Choppers, 8 out

Forks: Telescopic, 10 inches over

Rake: 65 degrees

Rear susp.: Hardtail

Front wheel: Performance Machine, 21-inch

Front brake: Performance Machine, disc

Rear wheel: Performance Machine, 18-inch

Rear Tire: 240 mm

Rear brake: Performance Machine disc/pulley

Engine: 124 cubic inch w/supercharger, nitrous-oxide injection

Exhaust: Thee Darkside of Daytona

Trans.: Baker 6-speed, hand shift

Paint by: Got 2B Kustom

Low Blow

Above: What looks like a nuclear powerplant is really a supercharged V-twin with nitrous-oxide injection that puts out only slightly less energy.

Below: Spined tail behind the seat encourages a strong grasp on the bars when the power is cut loose. Note the arrow-shaped rear frame section.

Above: Dried Blood Red paint covers the whole bike, with the fuel tank circled by a ring of skulls. The laughing gas is stored in a pair of cylinders residing just beneath the fuel tank.

Hard to believe, but this radical chopper began life as a Harley-Davidson—albeit a wrecked one. Bill Steel was the artisan who transformed the pile of parts into the striking machine seen here.

Actually, about the only Harley components used were the 88-cubic-inch Twin Cam 88B engine and its attendant 5-speed transmission. The bent frame was replaced by a chassis from Goldammer, which included inverted forks in front and a single-sided RC Components swingarm in back. Both ends feature adjustable air suspension, the compressed air being stored in the frame tubes.

The fuel tank came from the catalog of Paul Yaffe, but was modified to blend into the surrounding custom sheetmetal. Both front and rear fenders, along with the oil-tank surround, were hand-formed by Bill Steel. RC Components supplied the wheels and the rear brake disc/pulley, which, along with the single-sided swingarm, allows the right side of the wheel to run completely free of obstruction.

Yes, it's hard to believe this grew out of a wreck. And it has certainly come a long way from Milwaukee....

Right: Smoothed fork legs from Goldammer really stand out. Note that even the perch for the headlight is flushed into its surroundings.

Left: All cables and wires run inside the handlebars for a cleaner look. Tiny rearview mirror on the left bar-end is enough to make the bike legal. *Bottom, left:* The Harley-Davidson 88-cubic-inch V-twin is polished and fitted with custom intake and exhaust.

Single-sided swingarm and combination brake disc/pulley from RC Components allows a clear view of the mag-style wheel from the right side.

SPECIFICATIONS

Owner: Chuck Liptak

Builder: Bill Steel

Model: U-Bet 2

Frame: Goldammer, 5 up, 3 out

Forks: Goldammer, inverted, 10 inches over, with adjustable air suspension

Rake: 47 degrees

Rear susp.: Single-sided swingarm with adjustable air suspension

Front wheel: RC Components, 21-inch

Front brake: RC Components, disc

Rear wheel: RC Components, 18-inch

Rear tire: 250 mm

Rear brake: RC Components, disc/pulley

Engine: 88-cubic-inch Harley-Davidson

Exhaust: Hot Match

Trans.: Harley-Davidson, 5-speed

Paint by: Bill Steel

Revenge

year: 2004
builder: Midwest Choppers
class: Radical

First shown at the Laughlin River Run in 2004, Revenge drew the attention of several major cycle publications, and will likely be featured in an upcoming issue. Midwest Choppers built the bike for Scott Rives, and both are pleased with the outcome.

Ten-inch-over inverted forks set at a 46-degree rake combined with a stretched Midwest Choppers frame results in a posture that is anything but subtle. What is subtle, however, are the complex tribal graphics accenting Revenge's Candy Blue paintwork.

Somewhat unusual for a radical chopper is the Harley-Davidson Softail-style triangulated swingarm, which mimics the look of a hardtail frame while affording vastly greater comfort; it pivots at the top, extending a pair of shocks mounted beneath the engine. More common is the potent 124-cubic-inch S&S V-twin fitted with a Martin Bros. exhaust and Midwest Choppers' signature Maltese-cross air cleaner.

SPECIFICATIONS

Owner: Scott Rives

Builder: Midwest Choppers

Model: Revenge

Frame: Midwest Choppers, 6 up, 5 out

Forks: American Suspension, inverted, 10 inches over

Rake: 46 degrees

Rear susp.: Triangulated swingarm

Front wheel: Xtreme Machine, 21-inch

Front brake: American Suspension, disc

Rear wheel: Xtreme Machine, 18-inch

Rear tire: 250 mm

Rear brake: HHI, inboard disc/pulley

Engine: 124-cubic-inch S&S

Exhaust: Martin Bros.

Trans.: Jim's 6-speed

Paint by: Brian's Kustom Paint

It's difficult to make out the tribal flames accenting the Candy Blue paint, but that's part of the idea; subtlety lends a touch of elegance to the bike's clean lines. The triangulated swingarm hosts an Xtreme Machine wheel fitted with an HHI brake disc mounted inboard of the drive-belt pulley. Both the rear fender and exhaust tips are accented with pointed trailing edges.

Rock Hard

year: 2005
builder: Midwest Choppers/Rock Hymes
class: Radical

SPECIFICATIONS

Owner: Rock Hymes

Builder: Midwest Choppers/
Rock Hymes

Model: Rock Hard

Frame: Midwest Choppers,
9 up, 6 out

Forks: American Suspension,
inverted, 24 inches over

Rake: 51 degrees

Rear susp.: Swingarm

Front wheel: Xtreme Machine, 21-inch

Front brake: American Suspension,
disc

Rear wheel: Xtreme Machine, 18-inch

Rear tire: 300 mm

Rear brake: HHI, inboard disc/pulley

Engine: 124-cubic-inch S&S

Exhaust: Vance & Hines

Trans.: 6-speed, right-side drive

Paint by: Jeremy Imming

Rock Hymes wanted to build a unique chopper, but lacked some of the skills and tools required, so he approached Midwest Choppers about doing a cobuild. Rock had been impressed by the machines built by Midwest over the years, and the company was eager to be part of his team. Rock did some of the fabrication himself, drawing on Midwest's expertise when required.

The radical 51-degree rake joins with forks that are 24 inches over to throw the front end both up and out to nearly unprecedented proportions. Yet despite the extreme numbers, Rock Hard is easily ridden both on the highway and around town.

Power comes courtesy of a 124-cubic-inch S&S engine fitted with Vance & Hines exhaust and

Midwest Choppers' trademark Maltese-cross air cleaner. Xtreme Machine rims roll at both ends, the rear being fitted with an enormous 300-series tire for ample traction.

Flame paint jobs are common, but not the type of "real" flame treatment given to Rock Hard. By using less-defined edging on the flames, they seem to roll and flow, much like the real thing.

Rock Hard

Though Rock Hard is radical from stem to stern, it's the paint and body sculpting that really stand out. Soft, undefined edges on the flames put them in stark contrast to the sharply defined silver "blades" sharing space on the sculpted sheetmetal.

Tony

year: 2003
builder: Midwest Choppers
class: Radical

Tony, named after its owner, is the second bike Tony Morrow has had built by Midwest Choppers. So confident is he in the company's abilities that he gives it free reign in design and assembly. And that confidence has been rewarded. Tony is a spare, minimalist design that runs as good as it looks.

Ten-inch-over Spyke inverted forks set at a 46-degree rake give a radical appearance without sacrificing cornering ability. A swingarm rear suspension keeps the bumps at bay. Wheels made in a cooperative effort between Pro-Street and Frameworks extend their three-

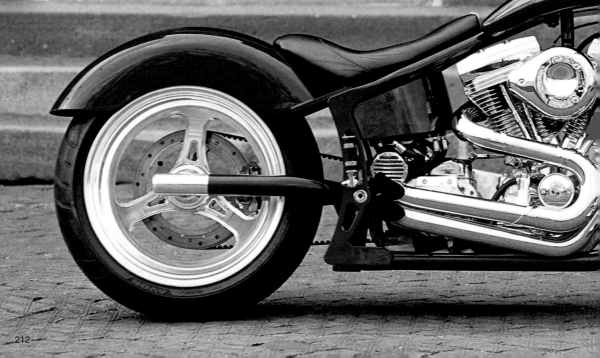

spoke design to the brake-disc hubs; in back, the disc sits inboard of the drive-belt pulley.

A 113-cubic-inch engine by El Bruto is accented with pieces by S&S and Midwest Choppers, with exhaust exiting through a pair of Yaffe Crack Pipes. The Candy Red paint is highlighted by subtle flame graphics that are hard to see in these photos; the allure of Tony, however, is not.

Tony

SPECIFICATIONS

Owner:	Tony Morrow
Builder:	Midwest Choppers
Model:	Tony
Frame:	Midwest Choppers, 6 up, 5 out
Forks:	Spyke, inverted, 10 inches over
Rake:	46 degrees
Rear susp.:	Swingarm
Front wheel:	Pro-Street/ Frameworks, 21-inch
Front brake:	HHI, disc
Rear wheel:	Pro-Street/ Frameworks, 18-inch
Rear tire:	250 mm
Rear brake:	HHI, inboard disc/pulley
Engine:	113-cubic-inch El Bruto
Exhaust:	Yaffe Crack Pipes
Trans.:	Jim's 6-speed
Paint by:	Ron Folger

Most choppers use primary (engine to transmission) belt drive; the belt doesn't require lubrication as would a chain, which eliminates oil drips. It also just looks cool. In most cases, the secondary (transmission to rear wheel) drive is also by belt—for the same reason. Yaffe Crack Pipes dress up the 113-cubic-inch El Bruto V-twin.

Opposite page: Symmetrical "half moon" rear fender topping a three-spoke wheel lends a simple, clean look to Tony. So does the subtle paintwork. Note the spiral fuel cap.

Deranged

Mick White has been a frequent customer of Midwest Choppers, and for his latest purchase he wanted something a little different. By combining radical front-end geometry with sculpted sheetmetal covered in vibrant graphics, Mick got the look he wanted.

Adding a little pizzazz of its own is a 124-cubic-inch S&S engine that's been diamond-cut for extra dazzle. A Maltese-cross air cleaner by Midwest Choppers

216

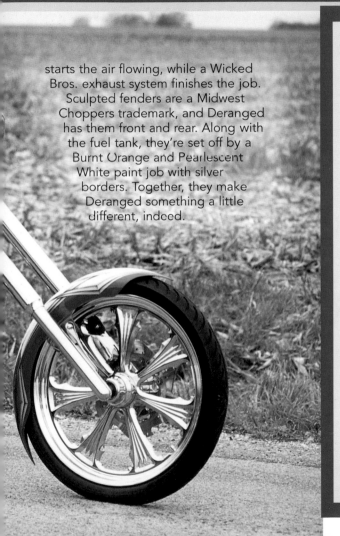

starts the air flowing, while a Wicked Bros. exhaust system finishes the job. Sculpted fenders are a Midwest Choppers trademark, and Deranged has them front and rear. Along with the fuel tank, they're set off by a Burnt Orange and Pearlescent White paint job with silver borders. Together, they make Deranged something a little different, indeed.

SPECIFICATIONS

Owner: Mick White

Builder: Midwest Choppers

Model: Deranged

Frame: Midwest Choppers, 5 up, 6 out

Forks: American Suspension, inverted, 12 inches over

Rake: 46 degrees

Rear susp.: Swingarm

Front wheel: Xtreme Machine, 21-inch

Front brake: American Suspension, disc

Rear wheel: Xtreme Machine, 18-inch

Rear tire: 300 mm

Rear brake: American Suspension, inboard disc/pulley

Engine: 124-cubic-inch S&S

Exhaust: Wicked Bros.

Trans.: 6-speed, right-side drive

Paint by: Jeremy Imming

Left: The trailing edges of both the front and rear fenders feature Midwest Choppers' signature "fangs." Silver highlighting accentuates the sculpting.
Above: Check out the fins on the cylinders and you'll see the scalloped look of the diamond-cut process. It's touches like this that really set a radical chopper apart from the crowd.

El Balla

John Dodson's racing experience and passion for fast motorcycles led to the creation of this, his first custom chopper. It also led to the creation of his company, Johnny Legend Customs.

An RC Components frame hosts American inverted forks raked at 48 degrees. Also from RC Components came a single-sided swingarm and combination brake disc/drive pulley that allow a clear view of the right side of the rear wheel. The front wheel and brake were also supplied by RC Components. Rear air suspension provides an adjustable ride height, allowing the bike to be lowered for "show" and raised for "go."

And go it does, thanks to a 124-cubic-inch V-twin from Total Performance. Pipes from Sampson complete the picture.

Custom-formed bodywork accents the frame and encloses the oil tank. But the focal point is the rear fender, which encapsulates a taillight between staggered layers of sheet-metal. Of course, some might argue the orange and purple paint scheme is what first draws the eye, but either way, it's obvious Johnny Legend Customs is off to a great start.

El Balla

SPECIFICATIONS

Owner: John Dodson

Builder: Johnny Legend Customs

Model: El Balla

Frame: RC Components, 6 out

Forks: American, inverted, 2 inches over

Rake: 48 degrees

Rear susp.: RC Components, single-sided swingarm with adjustable air suspension

Front wheel: RC Components, 21 inch

Front brake: RC Components, disc

Rear wheel: RC Components, 18 inch

Rear tire: 250mm

Rear brake: RC Components disc/pulley

Engine: 124-cubic-inch Total Performance

Exhaust: Sampson

Trans.: 5-speed

Paint by: Coles Auto Body

Right: Taillight is sandwiched between double-decker layers of the sculpted rear fender.

Opposite page: Inverted forks feature an internal brake line hidden within the left-side tube, a nice touch. **Left:** Single-sided swingarm and combination brake disc/ drive pulley allow the right side of the rear wheel to run "naked."

Thugster

year: 2002
builder: X-Treme Cycle/John Lewis
class: Radical

SPECIFICATIONS

Owner: John Lewis

Builder: X-Treme Cycle/John Lewis

Model: Thugster

Frame: X-Treme Cycle, 12 up

Forks: Perse, telescopic, 13 inches over

Rake: 40 degrees

Rear susp.: Hardtail

Front wheel: Spoke, 21 inch

Front brake: None

Rear wheel: Dayton automotive rim, 16 inch

Rear tire: 250 mm

Rear brake: X-Treme Cycle, disc/ sprocket

Engine: 80-cubic-inch Harley-Davidson

Exhaust: X-Treme Cycle

Trans.: 5-speed, hand shift

Paint by: Pro Body and Paint/ Striping by Liza

Despite his nickname, "Lil' John" Lewis of X-Treme Cycle has some big ideas. Though capable of building anything a client wants, he prefers ground-up customs like the Thugster shown here.

Using his skills and frame jigs, John bends tubing to create his own chassis, which gives him the ability to roll out any geometry that best suits the customer's needs. In this case, a 12-inch downtube stretch was matched with a rather upright 40-degree fork rake to provide an unusual profile—and better around-town handling. Perse telescopic

forks hold a spoke wheel devoid of brake clutter.

An unusual styling feature is the "see-through" fuel tank. John also bends and welds all of his own tanks, thus minimizing the possibility of running across anything like them on the street. Ditto his control-free handlebars, which appear to be just empty tubes. Multicolored metalflake paint adds visual appeal, as do accents that highlight details that might otherwise escape the untrained eye.

An 80-cubic-inch Harley-Davidson Evo engine powers the Thugster. The organ-pipe intake is an X-Treme Cycle original, as is the unique exhaust system. Another unusual touch is the rear brake pedal that does double duty as the clutch control: Depress the pedal halfway, and the clutch is disengaged; depress it all the way, and the rear brake is activated.

Throughout, the Thugster is loaded with innovative ideas—which is just one of the advantages of being able to build a bike your own way.

Thugster

A reliable, 80-cubic-inch Harley-Davidson Evo V-twin powers the Thugster, with help from a custom-bent exhaust and organ-pipe intake. Situated behind the engine is the oil tank, one of the many items John created himself.

Other X-Treme Cycle creations include the see-through fuel tank and hollow, lever-free handlebars. A skull knob tops the hand-shift lever.

Daddy Long Legs

Daddy Long Legs is aptly named, as it was built for a former Corn Huskers football player. Klock Werks, of Mitchell, South Dakota, designed the frame, placing the seat and forward controls to accommodate the big rider's physique.

The fuel tank started life as a standard West Coast Choppers item, but was modified for the application. Works Shocks cushion the triangulated swingarm in back, while Dakota Billet axles team with stretched, Harley-Davidson Deuce forks in front. Sixty-spoke wheels at both ends lend an "old school" look. A combination sprocket and brake disc by Exile mounts on the left side of the bike, allowing the right side of the wheel to run "open."

A 120-cubic-inch Patrick V-twin powers the big Daddy, with exhaust pipes specially bent by Klock Werks. Satin black paint contrasts with the normal high-gloss paintwork of most choppers, and is accented with strategically placed red and white pinstripes.

What the owner wanted was a specially sized bike with a unique look, and Klock Werks was happy to oblige—which is the whole idea behind these custom-built machines.

Daddy Long Legs

SPECIFICATIONS

Owner: Terry Eyman

Builder: Klock Werks

Model: Daddy Long Legs

Frame: Klock Werks, 6 up, 2 out

Forks: Harley-Davidson Deuce, telescopic, 10 inches over

Rake: 40 degrees

Rear susp.: Triangulated swingarm

Front wheel: Spoke, 21-inch

Front brake: Disc

Rear wheel: Spoke, 18-inch

Rear tire: 200 mm

Rear brake: Exile disc/sprocket

Engine: 120-cubic-inch Patrick

Exhaust: Klock Werks

Trans.: Rev Tech 6-speed

Paint by: Klock Werks

Below: Red-and-white pinstriping stands out against an unusual satin-black background.

Below: Specially bent pipes add another distinctive touch. Foot controls are set far forward to accommodate a tall ride

Chopsmiths may be a new venture, but judging by this custom-built machine, it will be producing choppers for many years to come. J. L. Hart is the craftsman behind most of the company's creations, and his talent is matched only by his imagination.

Starting with a CMC frame incorporating a triangulated swingarm, both the bottom and rear sections were altered to fit the desired profile. Springer forks, originally from a 1932 Harley-Davidson, were also modified for use on Shovelglide. Fuel and oil tanks were both hand formed by Chopsmiths, as was the rear fender. The headlight was created out of a piston from a John Deere tractor; the taillight came from an early Ford automobile.

The 88-cubic-inch engine was built-up from a variety of parts: Delkron cases, S&S cylinders, and STD heads. Exhaust pipes exit on each side of the bike and are wrapped in protective tape. A modern belt-drive primary is used, but an old-style foot clutch/hand shifter are brought into play to stir the gears.

Shovelglide's mixture of new technology, old-school design, hand-formed parts, and artistic imagination is a fitting tribute to its creator. The future of J. L. Hart and Chopsmiths looks bright, indeed.

SPECIFICATIONS

Owner:	Bethany Root
Builder:	Chopsmiths
Model:	Shovelglide
Frame:	CMC/Chopsmiths
Forks:	Harley-Davidson springer
Rake:	32 degrees
Rear susp.:	Triangulated swingarm
Front wheel:	Spoke, 16-inch
Front brake:	none
Rear wheel:	Spoke, 16-inch
Rear tire:	130 mm
Rear brake:	Disc
Engine:	88-cubic-inch Delkron/S&S/STD
Exhaust:	Chopsmiths
Trans.:	Delkron, 5-speed, hand shift
Paint by:	T.K./J.Cox

Shovelglide

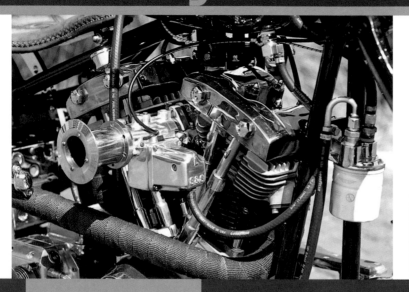

Below:
Taillight
is from an
old Ford
automobile.

Above: The engine's
valve covers
duplicate those of
a Harley-Davidson
Shovelhead
V-twin, but are tinted
gold, matching the
hand-turned velocity
stack on the S&S
carburetor.

Above: Perched atop the fuel tank with its "Shovelglide" logo is the hand-formed oil tank—tinted gold to match other trim on the bike. Note the wood handgrips that match the wood floorboards.

In the world of choppers, Thee Darkside of Daytona has a well-earned reputation for going above and beyond the typical build. Whether in the powertrain or the configuration, something is always done in the extreme.

Girder Chopper is based on a Killer Choppers hardtail frame, which has been modified in nearly every dimension, with a 6-inch stretch, 10-inch rise, and a 55-degree fork rake. Girder forks were stretched 22 inches for the profile Thee Darkside wanted. Spoke wheels reside at each end. The front one rides without a brake; in back, a Hawg Halters disc is used, as is a 250-series tire. Power comes courtesy of a 117-cubic-inch Ultima V-twin fitted with a "snaked" exhaust system bent by Thee Darkside.

The entire bike, including chassis and sheetmetal, was then cloaked in black, which strikes a stunning contrast to the chromed pieces. It all flows together to form a chopper befitting Thee Darkside's brand.

237

Girder Chopper

Left and below: Snaked exhaust pipes, hand-bent by the builder, add a distinctive look to the Girder Chopper; so does the machined primary "cover." *Right:* Spired handgrips and machined mirror mounts lend their own custom touch.

SPECIFICATIONS

Owner: Ashley Bailey

Builder: Thee Darkside
of Daytona

Model: Girder Chopper

Frame: Killer Choppers,
10 up, 6 out

Forks: Springer, 22 inches
over

Rake: 55 degrees

Rear susp.: Hardtail

Front wheel: Spoke, 21-inch

Front brake: None

Rear wheel: Spoke, 18-inch

Rear Tire: 250 mm

Rear brake: Hawg Halters, disc

Engine: 117-cubic-inch Ultima

Exhaust: Thee Darkside of
Daytona

Trans.: Delkron 5-speed

Paint by: Got 2B Kustom

Above: The Girder Chopper gets it name from
its stretched girder forks, which pivot up and
down on short arms to compress a coil-over
shock mounted behind the headlight. Not
many choppers use this style of forks.

Chopper, Baby

Steve Schaeffer has been building custom choppers for more than a decade, and this recent creation shows off his considerable talents.

A Chicago Chopper Works hardtail frame was chosen to support a set of 18-inch-over Redneck springer forks set at a whopping 52-degree rake, resulting in a striking profile. Black Bike wheels, each densely packed with 120 spokes, add to the radical look. A Performance Machine disc brake up front and a combination disc/sprocket from Exile at the rear provide the stopping power.

Adding a vintage touch is a 93-cubic-inch engine from Accurate Engineering. It's designed to look like a Harley-Davidson "Panhead"

V-twin from the 1950s, but offers modern reliability and considerably more power. To further distinguish his chopper, Steve bent up a set of custom-made pipes for the Panhead that snake out the left side rather than the right. Also unusual is the hand-shift/foot-clutch arrangement to stir the 6-speed transmission.

Though the fuel tank is a catalog item, it has been modified with a spine that runs front-to-back along the top. The seat is frenched into a custom-made rear fender. Other pieces made by Schaeffer include the handlebars, foot controls, and elaborately machined shift lever, all evidence of his undeniable skill.

SPECIFICATIONS

Owner: Steve Schaeffer

Builder: Schaef's Custom Cycles

Model: Chopper, Baby

Frame: Chicago Chopper Works, 5 up, 3 out

Forks: Redneck, springer, 18 inches over

Rake: 52 degrees

Rear susp.: Hardtail

Front wheel: Black Bike, 21-inch

Front brake: Performance Machine, disc

Rear wheel: Black Bike, 16-inch

Rear tire: 280 mm

Rear brake: Exile, disc/sprocket

Engine: 93-cubic-inch Accurate Engineering

Exhaust: Steve Schaeffer

Trans.: Baker 6-speed, hand shift

Paint by: Striping by Liza/ Will Christman

Above: Built by Accurate Engineering, the engine is fashioned after a Harley-Davidson "Panhead" V-twin of the '50s, which got the nickname because its valve covers looked like upside-down roasting pans.

Above: A distinctive look added by the builder is the red edging on the engine's cooling fins, which contrasts with the black-painted cylinders.

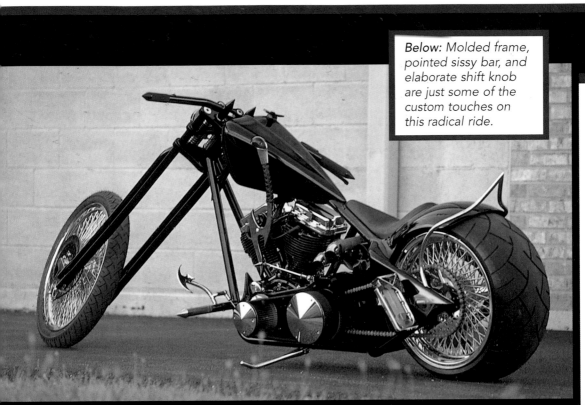

Below: Molded frame, pointed sissy bar, and elaborate shift knob are just some of the custom touches on this radical ride.

243

Joshua Ford has a preoccupation with pre-1950 artifacts, and this obsession influenced his latest creation. Built by his company, Killer Choppers, Fiend embodies many design themes Joshua finds intriguing, and the final product is far from ordinary.

Killer Choppers built a custom hardtail frame, fitting it with a springer fork bathed in black. Black Bike spoked wheels are fitted to both ends: In front, a 21-incher wraps around a Pat Kennedy disc brake; at the rear, a 16-incher mates to an Exile disc brake with integrated sprocket, all nestling beneath a ventilated fender.

Harley-Davidsons of the 1950s used a Panhead V-twin, and so does the Fiend—though this one benefits from S&S internal hardware resulting in 93 cubic inches of displacement. Spark is provided by a Morris magneto—another throwback to the '50s—to maintain a vintage look. The original 4-speed transmission gets an extra cog to provide five forward gears.

The low front end culminates in clip-on handlebars inspired by

older racing bikes. Spiderwebbing accents the Green Priznatique paint, and it all combines for a unique look that satisfies Joshua's nostalgic appetite.

SPECIFICATIONS

Owner: Joshua Ford

Builder: Killer Choppers

Model: Fiend

Frame: Killer Choppers, 4 down

Forks: Springer

Rake: 49 degrees

Rear susp.: Hardtail

Front wheel: Black Bike, 21-inch

Front brake: Pat Kennedy, disc

Rear wheel: Black Bike, 16-inch

Rear tire: 240 mm

Rear brake: Exile, disc/sprocket

Engine: 93-cubic-inch Harley-Davidson Panhead

Exhaust: Killer Choppers

Trans.: 5-speed

Paint by: Bonehead Design

Left: Clip-on handlebars, which clamp right to the fork tubes, provide an unusual look, both from an observer's and driver's perspective.

Opposite page, bottom: The Harley-Davidson Panhead engine hails from the '50s, but received modern internal components—and 93 cubic inches of displacement. Morris magneto beside the front cylinder provides spark, 1950s style.

Right: Spiderwebs—
a custom touch emanating
from the '50s—highlight
the fender portholes. Note
the STOP light; this, too, is
a vintage item.

247

Sabre Tooth

year: 2004
builder: Fearless Choppers
class: Radical

Fearless Choppers has but one goal: to build high-end machines with no equal. Regardless of the approach chosen, the end product will be as individual as the buyer.

Sabre Tooth rides a Precious Metal Customs chassis with 6-inch rise, 5-inch stretch, 52-degree rake on the forks, and a 300-mm rear tire. Motive force comes courtesy of a 114-cubic-inch V-twin from Powerhouse coupled to a Baker 6-speed transmission with right-side drive. Large-diameter tubing was bent by Creative Cycles to create a two-into-one exhaust system. Hawg Halter disc brakes slow both Xtreme Machine wheels.

Every inch of sheetmetal was hand-formed by Fearless Choppers and Precious Metal Customs to create a truly individual machine. Adding to its unique character are a flush-mounted fuel cap and machined metal handlebars, and it all goes together to make Sabre Tooth a fine example of the radical machines rolling out the doors of Fearless Choppers.

Sabre Tooth

SPECIFICATIONS

Owner: Martin Dring

Builder: Fearless Choppers

Model: Sabre Tooth

Frame: Precious Metal Customs, 6 up, 5 out

Forks: Mean Street, inverted, 26 inches over

Rake: 52 degrees

Rear susp.: Hardtail

Front wheel: Xtreme Machine, 21-inch

Front brake: Hawg Halters, disc

Rear wheel: Xtreme Machine, 18-inch

Rear tire: 300 mm

Rear brake: Hawg Halters, disc

Engine: 114-cubic-inch Powerhouse

Exhaust: Creative Cycles

Trans.: Baker 6-speed, right-side drive

Paint by: Davey Macks Paintworks

Unique, custom-formed fuel tank features a flush-mounted fuel cap on its left side. Note the machined billet handlebars. By contrast, the snakeskin seat, while exotic, is hardly unusual among Precious Metal Customs choppers.

Spoon Cobra

year: 2004
builder: Fearless Choppers
class: Radical

Martin Dring of Fearless Choppers and Russ Austin of Precious Metal Customs combined their considerable talents to build the Spoon Cobra. With its sculpted sheetmetal and distinctive touches, it was obviously a successful venture.

Beginning with a Precious Metal Customs chassis with 6-inch rise and 5-inch stretch, a 52-degree rake was applied to 24-inch-over forks from Mean Street. Weld wheels were used front and rear, both fitted with Hawg Halter disc brakes. A 280-series rear tire receives power

from a 96-cubic-inch S&S engine via a Baker 5-speed transmission with right-side drive.

Every inch of sheetmetal was hand-formed by Fearless Choppers and Precious Metal Customs, creating a truly individual machine. Candy Brandywine paint is highlighted with subtle images, the largest of which covers the top of the concave-sided fuel tank. The end result is a radical chopper that clearly shows what these combined forces can achieve.

Spoon Cobra

SPECIFICATIONS

Owner: Anthony Bonavolonta

Builder: Fearless Choppers

Model: Spoon Cobra

Frame: Precious Metal Customs, 6 up, 5 out

Forks: Mean Street, inverted, 24 inches over

Rake: 52 degrees

Rear susp.: Hardtail

Front wheel: Weld, 21-inch

Front brake: Hawg Halters, disc

Rear wheel: Weld, 18-inch

Rear tire: 280 mm

Rear brake: Hawg Halters, disc

Engine: 96-cubic-inch S&S

Exhaust: Creative Cycles

Trans.: Baker 5-speed, right-side drive

Paint by: Rick's Superpaint

Concave sides and custom fit make clear the fuel tank is no off-the-shelf component. Subtle but elaborate artwork gracing its top is more visible to the rider than to onlookers.

Top, left: Thinly padded, snakeskin-covered saddle adds another custom touch, but likely does little to absorb road shock passed on through the hardtail frame.
Left: An extreme 24-inch stretch allows the gracefully tapered inverted forks by Mean Street to be raked at a radical 52 degrees.

Fendered Spoon

Although Fearless Choppers has forged a reputation for building high-end machines, they are still capable of serving clients with less lofty goals. This Fendered Spoon model was the first to be built by Fearless Choppers with a rear fender, beneath which rolls a giant 300-mm tire.

The starting point was a Precious Metal Customs frame stretched 6 inches up, 5 inches out. To that, 16-inch-over American Suspension inverted forks were added, mounted at a 45-degree rake. Xtreme Machine wheels and Hawg Halters disc brakes are found on both axles.

The 80-cubic-inch engine is straight from Harley-Davidson, installed without modification or polishing.

year: 2004
builder: Fearless Choppers
class: Radical

Yet it still looks right at home in this custom chopper, despite having only a velocity stack and a set of Wicked Bros. exhaust pipes to dress it up.

Of course, no custom-built chopper would be complete without a grade-A paint job, and this one is no exception. A Cobalt Blue base coat enhanced with subtle ghost flames says "custom chopper" without screaming it—which is the whole idea behind this creation.

257

endered Spoon

SPECIFICATIONS

Owner: Frank Messina

Builder: Fearless Choppers

Model: Fendered Spoon

Frame: Precious Metal Customs, 6 up, 5 out

Forks: American Suspension, inverted, 16 inches over

Rake: 45 degrees

Rear susp.: Hardtail

Front wheel: Xtreme Machine, 21-inch

Front brake: Hawg Halters, disc

Rear wheel: Xtreme Machine, 18-inch

Rear tire: 300 mm

Rear brake: Hawg Halters, disc

Engine: 80-cubic-inch Harley-Davidson

Exhaust: Wicked Bros.

Trans.: Baker 5-speed, right-side drive

Paint by: Davey Macks Paintworks

Nearly all the aftermarket big-inch engines were modeled after this 80-cubic-inch Harley-Davidson "Evo" V-twin. Power output is more than adequate for the task, and the addition of a velocity stack on the carburetor and a set of custom pipes do wonders for the look.

Massive 300-mm rear tire is about as wide as they make for a chopper.

258

Mounting the headlight below the lower triple tree rather than above it, as is normal practice, alters the front-end appearance.

Ghost flames highlighting the Cobalt Blue paint are so subtle, they're hardly visible in these images...which is why they call them ghost flames.

Street Hustler

Building cookie-cutter, look-alike choppers is not what Kaotic Customs is all about. Every one of the company's machines is different from the last, the only constant being the pursuit of quality.

Street Hustler is built with hand-formed sheetmetal and custom-made handlebars carrying a sole instrument. The RC Components frame has a 38-degree rake in the neck, with another six degrees added by the triple trees for a total of 44 degrees. Adjustable air suspension acts on a triangulated swingarm at the rear to provide a comfortable ride. RC Components also sourced both the wheels and disc brakes. A 113-cubic-inch S&S engine exhales through Arlen Ness pipes.

It's difficult to categorize the paint scheme other than to say it defies convention. While the upper half of the bike seems cloaked in armor, the bottom half reflects a woodgrain theme. But it matches perfectly Kaotic Customs' creed that no two bikes look alike.

Above and left: Custom-made handlebars carry both wood and metal graphics. Armorlike paint scheme on the tank is accented with a "flaming skull" crest.

Right and opposite page, top: Scallops grace the edges of both fenders; in back, the scallops contain thin, frenched-in tail-lights.

Engine, oil tank, and lower frame are painted in a wood-grain motif. Custom air cleaner and Arlen Ness pipes with scalloped ends add a nice touch. Note the molded-in chin spoiler at the base of the frame.

SPECIFICATIONS

Owner: Kaotic Customs
Builder: Kaotic Customs
Model: Street Hustler
Frame: RC Components, 3 up, 2 out
Forks: RC Components, telescopic, 4 inches over
Rake: 44 degrees
Rear susp.: Triangulated swingarm w/adjustable air suspension
Front wheel: RC Components, 21-inch
Front brake: RC Components, disc
Rear wheel: RC Components, 18-inch
Rear tire: 250 mm
Rear brake: RC Components, disc
Engine: 113-cubic-inch S&S
Exhaust: Arlen Ness
Trans.: 6-speed
Paint by: Kaotic Customs/Fast and Furious

chopper

year: 2004
builder: Scooter Shooterz
class: Radical

SPECIFICATIONS

Owner: Dan Rodriguez

Builder: Scooter Shooterz

Model: Chopper

Frame: Diamond, 6 up, 5 out

Forks: Mean Street, telescopic, 12 inches over

Rake: 51 degrees

Rear susp.: Hardtail

Front wheel: Hallcraft, 21-inch

Front brake: RC Components/ Performance Machine, disc

Rear wheel: Hallcraft, 18-inch

Rear tire: 240 mm

Rear brake: RC Components/ Performance Machine, disc

Engine: 124-cubic-inch S&S

Exhaust: Scooter Shooterz

Trans.: Baker 5-speed, right-side drive

Paint by: Scooter Shooterz/ Jody Clark

Perhaps not as radical as some other Scooter Shooterz pieces, this bike is still a great example of what chopper building should be. A joint effort between the shop and the owner, it's a well-designed and well-executed machine.

The Diamond frame is stretched six inches up and five inches out for an aggressive stance, aided by Mean Street 12-inch-over forks set at a 51-degree rake. One-hundred-spoke wheels from

Hallcraft are coupled with brake rotors from RC Components and calipers from Performance Machine. A 124-cubic-inch S&S engine sports heads ported by Kendall Johnson for improved breathing and performance, sending its power through a Baker 5-speed transmission with right-side drive. The 240-series rear tire is conservative in this day of 300-mm skins, but allows for better handling.

A subtle combination of Galaxy Gray and silver metalflake paint blends nicely with chrome accents. Together, they provide a clean, almost stately look that makes this joint effort a joy to behold.

Chopper

Right and opposite page, top: Gray handlebars, frame, and trim accent the silver metalflake paint. Chromed teardrop headlight is a chopper mainstay.

S&S engine exhales through stubby, heat-wrapped exhaust pipes. Note the embroidery on the seat.

Spoke wheels give a classic look; sculpted rear fender is "classic" only in terms of radical choppers.

Executioner

year: 2004
builder: Scooter Shooterz
class: Radical

Scooter Shooterz built the Executioner for the Discovery Channel's popular Biker Build-Off program. The honor of being asked to participate is matched only by the creativity of the chopper entered.

Assembled in just nine days, the Executioner bristles with little custom touches—along with one blazing big one: a "head" light that spews flames from its gaping maw. Even without the fireworks, however, the bike is mighty impressive. Black paint carries gold-leaf accents, the rear fender is adorned with leather flames affixed with copper rivets, and the wheels are designed and cut by Scooter Shooterz itself.

The 107-cubic-inch engine features "Knucklehead"-style valve covers, a matte-black intake routed to the left side of the bike, and tape-wrapped exhaust. A pistol-grip hand shifter stirs the Baker 6-speed gearbox, leaving the clutch to be operated by a foot pedal. Legend air suspension allows the rider to adjust ride height at the rear, while Mean Street Warlord forks—featuring finely carved details—hold up the front.

But the highlight of the build is the flame-throwing, skull-shaped headlight. Lamps fill each eye socket, while the push of a button sends great waves of fire rolling from the open jaw. It certainly creates a spectacle, which is exactly what the Biker Build-Off program was all about.

SPECIFICATIONS

Owner: Warren Vesely

Builder: Scooter Shooterz

Model: Executioner

Frame: Scooter Shooterz, 8-inch stretch

Forks: Mean Street Warlord, telescopic, 12 inches over

Rake: 40 degrees

Rear susp.: Swingarm, Legend adjustable air suspension

Front wheel: Scooter Shooterz, 21-inch

Front brake: Disc

Rear wheel: Scooter Shooterz, 18-inch

Rear tire: 280 mm

Rear brake: Sprocket/disc

Engine: 107-cubic-inch V-twin w/Delkron heads

Exhaust: Scooter Shooterz

Trans.: Baker 6-speed, hand shift, right-side drive

Paint by: Scooter Shooterz/ Jody Clark

Executioner

Below: Seat and rear fender are set off by intricate leatherwork, a pistol-grip hand shifter picks the gears, and a chrome bottle stores fuel for the flamethrower. Left: Dressed for daytime, the "skull light" dons sunglasses. But come dark....

Opposite page: Lest the description "spews flames from its gaping maw" had you thinking Zippo lighter or propane torch, think again. Got marshmallows?

Lethal Injection

Scooter Shooterz has earned a reputation for building exotic choppers, but in terms of originality, Lethal Injection sets new standards. Proof of its allure came at a Louisville event, where it took Best Of Show honors.

At the heart of Lethal Injection is a 107-cubic-inch V-twin wearing 4-valve heads from Mega-Four and fed by a Hilborn mechanical fuel-injection system. Executed by Scooter Shooterz' own Warren Vesely, it performs even better than expected, overwhelming the massive 280-series rear tire under hard acceleration.

Oil for the engine is carried in the bike's frame downtube as well as externally mounted auxiliary storage tubes. Scooter Shooterz cut a pair of one-off wheels for Lethal Injection, and a GMA component does double duty as rear brake disc and drive pulley.

Every inch of the bodywork is original and the fuel tank sets

new standards for complexity. The chosen hue is Big Red Flake from the House Of Kolor, with silver-leaf accents and a seat embroidered with the bike's name adding custom touches to the high-powered beast.

SPECIFICATIONS

Owner: Warren Vesely

Builder: Scooter Shooterz

Model: Lethal Injection

Frame: Scooter Shooterz,
7 out

Forks: DNA springer,
4 inches over

Rake: 47 degrees

Rear susp.: Hardtail

Front wheel: Scooter Shooterz,
21-inch

Front brake: Performance Machine,
disc

Rear wheel: Scooter Shooterz,
18-inch

Rear tire: 280 mm

Rear brake: GMA disc/pulley

Engine: 107-cubic-inch V-twin
w/ 4-valve heads,
fuel injection

Exhaust: Scooter Shooterz

Trans.: Baker 6-speed,
right-side drive

Paint by: Scooter Shooterz/
Jody Clark

Lethal Injection

If the artful bodywork isn't enough to separate Lethal Injection from the crowd, its mighty four-valve fuel-injected V-twin should be. The intricacies of the Hilborn injection system make it a work of art on its own. Note the elaborately sculpted fuel tank.

Punisher

year: 2004
builder: The Wrench Custom Cycles
class: Radical

Punisher is the creation of The Wrench Custom Cycles. Nearly every aspect of this machine has been handcrafted, with innovations evident from virtually any view.

Punisher eschews the usual chrome trappings, instead adopting a sinister black-and-blue theme. TWCC's skull logo sneaks its way onto many of the bike's components, including artistic renderings on the fuel tank, along with cutouts on the primary-drive cover and between the handlebars.

Added to a TWCC-built frame are a set of American Suspension forks with a front brake caliper integrated into the lower leg and blacked-out tubes that play into the bike's color scheme. The front brake rotor bears the marks of TWCC's logo.

Blacked-out three-spoke wheels from Weld complete the chassis package.

Power comes courtesy of a 113-cubic-inch engine from Patrick, which matches the prevailing color scheme with blue cases and blacked-out cylinders. Following suit are the black heat-wrapped exhaust pipes and air-cleaner cover with TWCC logo. The Baker 6-speed transmission is shifted via a hand lever, while a foot pedal activates the clutch.

With its dark colors and lack of chrome, Punisher doesn't look like most other custom choppers. But then, maybe that's the point.

Punisher

SPECIFICATIONS

Owner: Brad Ruel

Builder: The Wrench Custom Cycles

Model: Punisher

Frame: The Wrench Custom Cycles, 8 up, 6 out

Forks: American Suspension, inverted, 14 inches over

Rake: 51 degrees

Rear susp.: Hardtail

Front wheel: Weld Wheels, 21-inch

Front brake: American Suspension, disc

Rear wheel: Weld Wheels, 18-inch

Rear tire: 280 mm

Rear brake: Exile, disc/sprocket

Engine: 113-cubic-inch Patrick

Exhaust: The Wrench Custom Cycles

Trans.: Baker 6-speed, handshift

Paint by: Eric Warren Designs

Above: *Black tribal flames look sinister against Punisher's sea of dark blue paint.*

Skull logo of The Wrench Custom Cycles appears on the seat, front brake disc, air-cleaner cover, and above the handlebars. Primary-drive cover sports it as well. **Left:** Note the short, black (of course) shift lever that's used to stir the gears by hand.

Turbo Spike

year: 2004
builder: Kaotic Customs
class: Radical

Based in Ft. Lauderdale, Florida, Kaotic Customs has designed and built numerous choppers for a variety of clients. No two have been alike, but a theme of high-quality fit and finish applies to every model sold.

As one might guess, Turbo Spike is powered by a boosted engine; in this case, a 100-cubic-inch S&S V-twin with Garrett turbocharger and exhaust plumbing bent by Kaotic Customs. The RC Components frame has been altered for the desired stance, with an air-adjustable triangulated swingarm in back and 14-inch-over inverted forks in front. Arlen Ness wheels with matching brake discs complete the chassis package. Topping it all off are bright red-and-yellow scorpion graphics on the sheetmetal, frame, and even the engine—a fitting paint scheme for a beautifully built chopper packing a turbocharged sting.

Turbo Spike

Turbocharging the 100-cubic-inch V-twin requires a host of plumbing. The intake is situated on the left side of the bike, while the exhaust routes first to the turbocharger, then snakes down through a single pipe. Note that frame and engine carry the same scorpion-themed paintwork as the sheetmetal.

SPECIFICATIONS

Owner:	Kaotic Customs
Builder:	Kaotic Customs
Model:	Turbo Spike
Frame:	RC Components/ Kaotic Customs, 8 up, 5 out
Forks:	RC Components, inverted, 14 inches over
Rake:	46 degrees
Rear susp.:	Triangulated swingarm w/adjustable air suspension
Front wheel:	Arlen Ness, 21-inch
Front brake:	RC Components, disc
Rear wheel:	Arlen Ness, 18-inch
Rear tire:	250 mm
Rear brake:	RC Components, disc
Engine:	100-cubic-inch S&S, turbocharged
Exhaust:	Kaotic Customs
Trans.:	Accurate 6-speed
Paint by:	Kaotic Customs/Fast and Furious

Hard Tail

year: 2004
builder: Ideal Ride/Tom Werner
class: Radical

No chopper owner wants to be seen on a ride that looks like any other. Fortunately, by combining catalog items with some creative imagination, almost any bike can end up being utterly unique.

Based on a frame from Accessories Unlimited, Hard Tail was fitted with 10-inch-over Mean Street inverted forks set at a 47-degree rake. Eighty spoke wheels dress each end, both carrying a disc brake; in back, the disc is part of the left-side drive sprocket, which allows the right side of the wheel to run "open." Driving that sprocket is a

6-speed transmission, itself driven by a 113-cubic-inch S&S engine with an exhaust system from Jesse James' West Coast Choppers.

Cobalt Blue paint covers the frame and all sheetmetal, the latter also sporting Candy Green flames. It's an unusual color combination to be sure, but that's the kind of "creative imagination" that makes this bike like no other.

Hard Tail

Whether in design or choice of colors, it's often the paint scheme that sets a chopper apart from the crowd. Brilliant Candy Green flames on a Cobalt Blue background should do the trick.

SPECIFICATIONS

Owner: Tom Warner

Builder: Ideal Ride/Tom Warner

Model: Hard Tail

Frame: Accessories Unlimited, 6 up, 6 out

Forks: Mean Street, inverted, 10 inches over

Rake: 47 degrees

Rear susp.: Hardtail

Front wheel: Spoke, 21-inch

Front brake: Performance Machine, disc

Rear wheel: Spoke, 18-inch

Rear tire: 250 mm

Rear brake: Exile, disc/sprocket

Engine: 113-cubic-inch S&S

Exhaust: Jesse James

Trans.: Accessories Unlimited, 6-speed

Paint by: Paint Spot

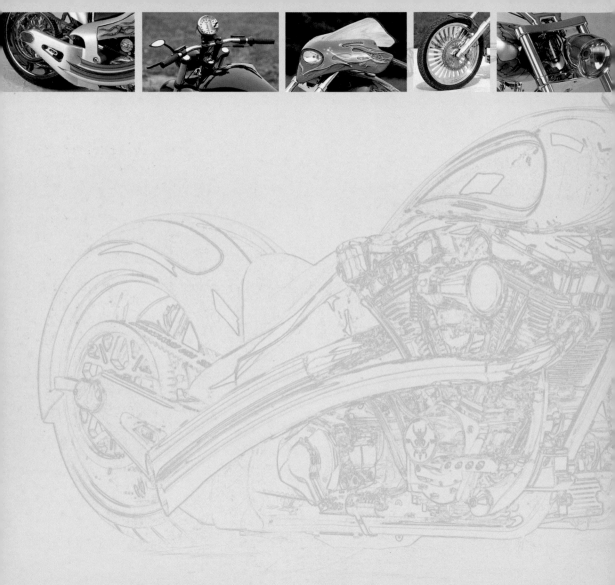

Oftentimes, there are only subtle differences between a Factory or Radical chopper and a Pro Street bike. Typically, Pro Streets are made to look—and run—like race bikes, which means they usually lack the raised frames, long forks, exotic detailing, and colorful paint schemes of their flashier siblings. Though there are exceptions—as you'll see—many feature a stark, austere appearance that gives them a purposeful look; that of a lean, mean, street-fighting machine.

PRO STREET

Dave Dupor of DD Custom Cycles is fast becoming one of the nation's hottest chopper builders. By combining the finest hardware with cutting-edge design and flawless workmanship, his machines are drawing the attention of buyers from across the country.

Many of today's choppers are lacking in the comfort and handling departments. But this one was built to satisfy the desire for a striking chopper that was also eminently drivable, and it rides as good as it looks.

The chassis consists of a swingarm frame from War Eagle hosting a set of Sunmyth forks. Added to that were full fenders that wrap around the tires, along with a fuel tank boasting subtle insets on both sides for a unique look.

Painted a two-tone scheme of Pearl Blue and Orient Blue, the colorful sheetmetal is closely matched by a set of blue-anodized Pro-One Sinister wheels. A diamond-cut finish on the 124 cubic-inch S&S engine adds even more sparkle to a machine that already draws its share of admiration.

PRO STREET

SPECIFICATIONS

Owner: Kenny Glick

Builder: DD Custom Cycles

Model: Pro Street

Frame: War Eagle, 2 out

Forks: Sunmyth, telescopic, 5 inches over

Rake: 42 degrees

Rear susp.: Swingarm w/air-adjustable suspension

Front wheel: Pro-One, 21-inch

Front brake: Disc

Rear wheel: Pro-One, 18-inch

Rear tire: 280 mm

Rear brake: Inboard disc/pulley

Engine: 124-cubic-inch S&S

Exhaust: DD Custom Cycles/ Thunder Cycle

Trans.: Rivera 6-speed, right-side drive

Paint by: MNK Custom Works

Opposite page, top: Fuel tank features inset side panels and is accented with contrasting pinstripes. *Bottom:* Cooling fins on the S&S V-twin are diamond-cut for added pizzazz. *This page:* Tires are enveloped by wraparound fenders; the rear one hosts a taillight frenched into its trailing edge.

CHECKERS

year: 1999
builder: Crown Custom Cycle Fabrications
class: Pro Street

Bud Dennis of Crown Custom Cycle Fabrications has a long-standing reputation for building high-performance Harley-Davidsons for the dragstrip. So it seems only natural he would eventually put his extraordinary knowledge to work on a street machine.

Though a Harley Softail model was the starting point, most major components have been replaced with more performance-oriented hardware. That includes the frame, purchased from Bourget Bike Works, needed to house the enlarged engine. Progressive supplied the rear suspension, but the original forks—shortened by two inches—hold up the front.

The heart of the beast is a hand-built 140-cubic-inch monster V-twin fed by twin S&S carburetors. And as if that weren't enough, there's also a nitrous oxide system onboard for added punch. Assigned to rein in all that power are dual Harley disc brakes in front and a single Performance Machine anchor in back.

Though "go" is certainly the name of the game here, "show" has not been ignored. An elaborate, brightly colored paint scheme combines with plenty of polished parts to turn heads as the bike goes by—most likely, very quickly.

CHECKERS

Twin carbs—one on each side of the bike—feed the hungry 140-cubic-inch V-twin, which eats nitrous for dessert; note the injectors in the left-side manifold just ahead of the cylinder.

Opposite page, right: Considering the power available, the Kosman rear wheel holds what seems to be a rather modest tire—with a very short life expectancy.

Colorful paint scheme adds show to the go.

SPECIFICATIONS

Owner: Bud Dennis

Builder: Crown Custom Cycle Fabrications (CCCF)

Model: Checkers

Frame: Bourget Bike Works, 2 out

Forks: Harley-Davidson, telescopic, 2 inches under

Rake: 40 degrees

Rear susp.: Progressive, swingarm

Front wheel: CCCF, 17-inch

Front brake: Harley-Davidson, dual disc

Rear wheel: Kosman, 18-inch

Rear tire: 180 mm

Rear brake: Performance Machine, disc

Engine: 140-cubic-inch hand-built V-twin

Exhaust: CCCF

Trans.: 5-speed

Paint by: Bud Dennis and Jim Brando

Based in a small town in Indiana, Scooter Shooterz is making a big name for itself. After showing its wares at a custom cycle show, the company was selected to participate in the hugely successful Biker Build-Off on The Discovery Channel.

Most of Scooter Shooterz's creations would fall under the Radical category, but this one, named Assassin, is considered a Pro Street bike. And it looks the part: The steel frame is constructed of substantial 2¼-inch tubing, forks are raked at a mild 38 degrees for crisp control, and the black exhaust pipes and engine cases lend a businesslike appearance.

But all show and no go is not the way Scooter Shooterz builds its bikes. To live up to its name, Assassin was fitted with a 124-cubic-inch S&S engine coupled to a 6-speed transmission—and fat 300-mm rear tire.

One of Scooter Shooterz's unusual talents is the ability to design and produce its own wheels. A pair of Executioner rims are used on the Assassin, one of many designs offered by the company.

ASSASSIN

SPECIFICATIONS

Owner: Larry Nagy

Builder: Scooter Shooterz

Model: Assassin

Frame: Assassin

Forks: Telescopic

Rake: 38 degrees

Rear susp.: Hardtail

Front wheel: Scooter Shooterz, 21-inch

Front brake: Performance Machine, disc

Rear wheel: Scooter Shooterz, 18-inch

Rear tire: 300 mm

Rear brake: Performance Machine, disc

Engine: 124-cubic-inch S&S

Exhaust: Scooter Shooterz

Trans.: 6-speed, right-side drive

Paint by: Scooter Shooterz

The Executioner is just one of many wheel styles offered by Scooter Shooterz, which designs them in-house.

Austere black headlight housing hints of this *Pro Street's* intended purpose; tachometer atop handlebars confirms it. So do the black engine cases and massive 300-mm rear tire.

PRO STREET

year: 2003
builder: Custom Shop Cycles
class: Pro Street

It was a charity raffle that prompted the construction of this colorful Pro Street machine. Built by Custom Shop Cycles, purveyors of high-end, high-performance bikes, it was no doubt appreciated by both the raffle winner and the charity.

The starting point was a Pro-One frame with unusual four-link rear suspension. All bodywork was handcrafted by John Wargo at Custom Shop Cycles, who is well-known for his ability to bend metal into complex shapes. John also applied the paintwork, with its striking flames and subtle images. Turbine-brand wheels roll at both ends, the rear being a solid disc. A 113-cubic-inch Ultima engine moves the colorful beast along, with its Sampson Boneshaker exhaust ensuring it doesn't go by unnoticed.

Construction took the better part of two months, but in the end, there were really three winners: the holder of the lucky ticket, the chosen charity, and the reputation of Custom Shop Cycles.

PRO STREET

Above: Elaborate bodywork includes sculpted rear fender and frenched-in driver and passenger seats. Below: Unusual 4-link rear suspension adds a hi-tech touch.

SPECIFICATIONS

Owner: Custom Shop Cycles

Builder: Custom Shop Cycles

Model: Pro Street

Frame: Pro-One, 1 up, 2 out

Forks: Pro-One, telescopic, 5 inches over

Rake: 43 degress

Rear susp.: Pro-One, four-link swingarm

Front wheel: Turbine, 21-inch

Front brake: HHI, disc

Rear wheel: Turbine, 18-inch

Rear tire: 240 mm

Rear brake: HHI, disc

Engine: 113-cubic-inch Ultima

Exhaust: Sampson Boneshaker

Trans.: Chrome Horse, 5-speed

Paint by: Custom Shop Cycles

SPEED DEMON

year: 2004
builder: DD Custom Cycles
class: Pro Street

Due to the high caliber of Dave Dupor's custom creations, clients often come back for a second helping. Such is the case with Speed Demon, as this is the second chopper Dave's DD Custom Cycles has built for the owner.

A stretched War Eagle frame with swingarm rear suspension holds two-inch-over Mean Street telescopic forks. Weld Wheels are found at both ends, each holding a matching disc brake; in back, the disc rides inboard of the drive pulley. A Rivera 6-speed right-side-drive transmission and 124-cubic-inch S&S engine exhaling through Martin Bros. pipes complete the chassis picture.

A fuel tank stretched to match the elongated frame is joined by formed fenders and oil tank to achieve a custom look, and they're all covered in silver paint accented with an exotic flame motif. The end result is a custom chopper that may well bring its two-time owner back for more.

Speed Demon

"Peaked" sculpting at the trailing edges of the frame and exhaust pipes mirrors the contours of the fenders. It's this type of integrated look that helps set a custom apart from the crowd.

SPECIFICATIONS

Owner: James Keith

Builder: DD Custom Cycles

Model: Speed Demon

Frame: War Eagle, 5 out

Forks: Mean Street,
telescopic,
5 inches over

Rake: 42 degrees

Rear susp.: Swingarm

Front wheel: Weld Wheels, 21-inch

Front brake: Disc

Rear wheel: Weld Wheels, 18-inch

Rear tire: 280 mm

Rear brake: Inboard disc/pulley

Engine: 124-cubic-inch S&S

Exhaust: Martin Bros.

Trans.: Rivera 6-speed,
right-side drive

Paint by: MNK Custom Works

BUELL STREET FIGHTER

Having seen his share of long-legged choppers, John Dawson decided to build a machine that was the polar opposite of the traditional custom. He wanted to put a torquey V-twin engine in a bike that handled as good as it looked.

Eric Buell founded the company that bears his name in the late 1980s on very much the same idea. He took Harley-Davidson Sportster engines and mounted them in exotic sport-style chassis, which resulted in bikes that were decidedly different than anything then being offered. Since that time, the Sportster engines Buell uses have been treated to significant changes that result in greatly increased power, but the chassis designs remain that of a high-riding "crotch rocket" sportbike.

So what John Dawson did was take a Buell motorcycle and swap its tall, sport-bike chassis for a low-slung hardtail frame by MC Worx. The original Buell forks and brakes were refitted, and John adapted a host of new hardware to create a low-slung bullet. Chief among them is a small bikini fairing incorporating twin headlights.

The result is a machine that bridges the rather wide gap between sportbikes and choppers. But in simplicity of design and unique treatment, John just did Eric Buell one better.

ERCHARGED

m Shop Cycles decided to build its first chopper, it went
full-blown crazy just to show the world what it could do.
ny has since gone on to build many extreme machines,
e still sets the pace.
g with a Paramount Cycles hardtail frame, six inches were
e backbone for a long, lean look. Pro-One forks hold a
l with HHI disc brake; in back, a matching rim is fitted
A disc/pulley. A 280-mm tire puts power to the road.
er this bike has—in spades. While a 113-cubic-
e is hardly extreme in today's chopper

311

BUELL STREET FIGHTER

SPECIFICATIONS

Owner: John Dawson

Builder: John Dawson

Model: Buell Street Fighter

Frame: MC Worx

Forks: Buell, inverted

Rake: 32 degrees

Rear susp.: Hardtail

Front wheel: PMSR, 18-inch

Front brake: Buell, disc

Rear wheel: PMSR, 18-inch

Rear tire: 240 mm

Rear brake: Buell, disc

Engine: 74-cubic-inch Buell

Exhaust: John Dawson

Trans.: Buell, 5-speed

Paint by: Greg Garcia

The MC Worx hardtail frame eliminates the Buell's complex rear suspension.

Left: *The 1200-cc (74-cubic-inch) Buell V-twin—a hopped-up version of a Harley-Davidson Sportster engine—received numerous upgrades to enhance performance even more. Short, "open" exhaust pipes delete the Buell's muffler, cutting weight and back-pressure.*

Once Custo
the route of
The compa
but this one
Beginnin
added to th
Weld whee
with a GM
And pow
inch engin

BUELL STREET FIGHTER

SPECIFICATIONS

Owner: John Dawson

Builder: John Dawson

Model: Buell Street Fighter

Frame: MC Worx

Forks: Buell, inverted

Rake: 32 degrees

Rear susp.: Hardtail

Front wheel: PMSR, 18-inch

Front brake: Buell, disc

Rear wheel: PMSR, 18-inch

Rear tire: 240 mm

Rear brake: Buell, disc

Engine: 74-cubic-inch Buell

Exhaust: John Dawson

Trans.: Buell, 5-speed

Paint by: Greg Garcia

The MC Worx hardtail frame eliminates the Buell's complex rear suspension.

Left: The 1200-cc (74-cubic-inch) Buell V-twin—a hopped-up version of a Harley-Davidson Sportster engine—received numerous upgrades to enhance performance even more. Short, "open" exhaust pipes delete the Buell's muffler, cutting weight and back-pressure.

SUPERCHARGED

year: 2004
builder: Custom Shop Cycles
class: Pro Street

Once Custom Shop Cycles decided to build its first chopper, it went the route of full-blown crazy just to show the world what it could do. The company has since gone on to build many extreme machines, but this one still sets the pace.

Beginning with a Paramount Cycles hardtail frame, six inches were added to the backbone for a long, lean look. Pro-One forks hold a Weld wheel with HHI disc brake; in back, a matching rim is fitted with a GMA disc/pulley. A 280-mm tire puts power to the road.

And power this bike has—in spades. While a 113-cubic-inch engine is hardly extreme in today's chopper

world, the addition of both a supercharger and nitrous oxide injection make a strong statement. So does the Hooker header when the ponies are cut loose.

Every inch of sheetmetal was formed by Custom Shop Cycles for this project, and over it, a multicolored paint scheme was applied.

After all, if a bike is to serve as your mobile masthead, you wouldn't want it to be all "go" and no "show."

SUPERCHARGED

The heart of this build—its reason for being—is its supercharged, nitrous-injected V-twin. The supercharger, sporting a cone-shaped intake, sits in front of the engine. At top right is the bright nitrous oxide storage cylinder with its red "Nos" label.

Left: Elaborate paint scheme dressing the tank shows the polish that backs up the punch.

Below: Rear fender features drilled "portholes" with a sliver of a taillight frenched into its trailing edge.

SPECIFICATIONS

Owner: Custom Shop Cycles

Builder: Custom Shop Cycles

Model: Supercharged

Frame: Paramount Cycles, 6 out

Forks: Pro-One, telescopic, 10 inches over

Rake: 46 degrees

Rear susp.: Hardtail

Front wheel: Weld Wheels, 21-inch

Front brake: HHI, disc

Rear wheel: Weld Wheels, 18-inch

Rear tire: 280 mm

Rear brake: GMA, disc/pulley

Engine: 113-cubic-inch S&S, supercharged

Exhaust: Hooker

Trans.: Accessories Unlimited, 5-speed

Paint by: Custom Shop Cycles

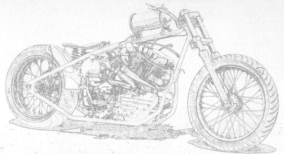

GLOSSARY

The world of choppers includes many words and terms that are not commonly used, or beg further explanation. Many of the following can be found in the text or specification charts in this book, and often come up in any discussion of choppers.

Aftermarket companies: Producers of parts and accessories that are designed to fit on a production vehicle, but the companies don't make the vehicles themselves. In the case of choppers, these parts can include small items, like seats and mirrors, and also large ones, such as engines, transmissions, and even frames. Since many aftermarket chopper companies got their start supplying replacement parts for Harley-Davidson motorcycles, their products often resemble Harley components.

Ape hangers: Tall handlebars.

Billet: Solid chunks of metal—usually a lightweight aluminum alloy—that are cut and milled to form parts such as brake arms, footpegs, and mirror mounts. The process of forming the billet is expensive, but results in a custom piece that looks far better than a standard component.

Brakes: Old-fashioned drum brakes are rare on choppers. Modern disc brakes have a large rotor that's gripped by a caliper; they work much the same way as hand brakes on a bicycle. Most motorcycles have the brake disc on one side of the rear wheel, the drive pulley (for a belt) or sprocket (for a chain) on the other side. But on some choppers, the rear disc is either part of the pulley or sprocket, or is mounted inboard on the same side of the wheel. This leaves the other side of the wheel "open," providing onlookers a better view of its fancy design.

Diamond-cut: Serrations cut into the edges of the engine's cylinder fins to make them sparkle in the light.

Engines: Most are V-twins patterned after those offered by Harley-Davidson over the years. They are built by aftermarket companies (see entry) such as S&S, Rev Tech, TP Engineering, and Ultima, and are usually larger and much more powerful than Harley's engines, which are still used in many choppers. Aftermarket engines usually mimic the look of Harley's Evolution (more commonly called "Evo") V-twin built from 1984 to 1999, but others are made to look like the Harley-Davidson "Panhead"of 1948-65, or the "Shovelhead" of 1966-84. The nicknames Panhead, Shovelhead, and the earlier Knucklehead

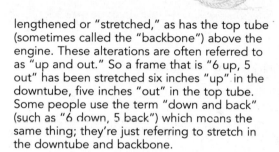

(1936-47) were all coined by riders—not Harley-Davidson—and referred to the look of the ngines' valve covers.

nal drive: The belt or chain that transfers power from the transmission to the rear wheel.

Forks: They generally come in four styles. *Telescopic:* Lower "sleeves" slide up and down n tubes, compressing internal coil springs. *Inverted:* the same, only upside down; the sleeves are at the top. *Springer:* The wheel moves up and down on short arms; long rods connected to the arms activate coil springs at the top. *Girder:* Solid forks move up and down on short arms at the top, compressing a spring. In most cases, the length of extended forks is based on the length of standard Harley-Davidson Softail forks, so if they're "10 inches over," they're 10 inches longer than stock Harley forks.

Frames: They're offered by numerous companies, but their dimensions are based on a stock Harley-Davidson Softail frame. Oftentimes, the downtube in front of the engine has been

lengthened or "stretched," as has the top tube (sometimes called the "backbone") above the engine. These alterations are often referred to as "up and out." So a frame that is "6 up, 5 out" has been stretched six inches "up" in the downtube, five inches "out" in the top tube. Some people use the term "down and back" (such as "6 down, 5 back") which means the same thing; they're just referring to stretch in the downtube and backbone.

Nitrous oxide: A gas that allows more fuel to be burned in the cylinders, resulting in more power. It is sometimes referred to as "laughing gas," as a purified form can be used as an anesthetic in surgery.

Primary drive: Often a belt, but sometimes a chain, that transfers power from the engine to the transmission. Most production motorcycles use chains, which are hidden behind covers that hold in the necessary lubricant. Most choppers use a three-inch-wide cogged belt, which requires no oil and thus no cover.

Rake: The angle of the forks, in degrees from vertical. The higher the number, the more the forks "stick out." The angle of the frame's neck determines most of the rake, but sometimes the triple trees (see entry) that hold the forks add even more rake.

Rear suspension: Many choppers are "hard-tails," meaning they have no rear suspension. Others have conventional swingarms—either straight tubes, tubes bent into a design, or tubes that form a triangle—acting on coil springs that are usually concealed, but sometimes visible.

Stepped seat: Also known as a "King and Queen" seat, it positions the passenger high above the rider, and was a defining element of choppers from the '60s and '70s.

Tires: Only the rear tire is mentioned because it's the one that varies the most in width. Most standard Harley-Davidsons come with rear tires that are 130-150 mm wide—about five to six inches. Some choppers have rear tires that are 300 mm wide (nearly the width of two pages of this book!), and recently, a company began offering a 360-mm tire.

Transmissions: Those built by aftermarket companies sometimes come with their final-drive sprockets or pulleys on the right side rather than the normal left-side placement. This is usually done in order to accommodate a very wide rear tire. (See *Tires*.) Most are conventional foot-shift transmissions with a hand-operated clutch, but some—as noted in the specification chart—are fitted with hand shifters and foot clutches, which were commonly used on motorcycles prior to the early 1950s.

Triple trees, or trees: Formed pieces that hold the fork legs, connecting them to the handlebars and frame neck. Some are designed to add more rake to the forks than is provided by the frame neck.

Wheels: Range from spoke-type that are relatively common and inexpensive, to one-off designs intricately milled from a solid disk of metal that can cost thousands of dollars apiece. In our specification charts, the latter usually include the supplier's name.

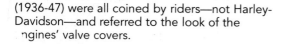

(1936-47) were all coined by riders—not Harley-Davidson—and referred to the look of the engines' valve covers.

nal drive: The belt or chain that transfers power from the transmission to the rear wheel.

Forks: They generally come in four styles. *Telescopic:* Lower "sleeves" slide up and down on tubes, compressing internal coil springs. *Inverted:* the same, only upside down; the sleeves are at the top. *Springer:* The wheel moves up and down on short arms; long rods connected to the arms activate coil springs at the top. *Girder:* Solid forks move up and down on short arms at the top, compressing a spring. In most cases, the length of extended forks is based on the length of standard Harley-Davidson Softail forks, so if they're "10 inches over," they're 10 inches longer than stock Harley forks.

Frames: They're offered by numerous companies, but their dimensions are based on a stock Harley-Davidson Softail frame. Oftentimes, the downtube in front of the engine has been

lengthened or "stretched," as has the top tube (sometimes called the "backbone") above the engine. These alterations are often referred to as "up and out." So a frame that is "6 up, 5 out" has been stretched six inches "up" in the downtube, five inches "out" in the top tube. Some people use the term "down and back" (such as "6 down, 5 back") which means the same thing; they're just referring to stretch in the downtube and backbone.

Nitrous oxide: A gas that allows more fuel to be burned in the cylinders, resulting in more power. It is sometimes referred to as "laughing gas," as a purified form can be used as an anesthetic in surgery.

Primary drive: Often a belt, but sometimes a chain, that transfers power from the engine to the transmission. Most production motorcycles use chains, which are hidden behind covers that hold in the necessary lubricant. Most choppers use a three-inch-wide cogged belt, which requires no oil and thus no cover.

Rake: The angle of the forks, in degrees from vertical. The higher the number, the more the forks "stick out." The angle of the frame's neck determines most of the rake, but sometimes the triple trees (see entry) that hold the forks add even more rake.

Rear suspension: Many choppers are "hard-tails," meaning they have no rear suspension. Others have conventional swingarms—either straight tubes, tubes bent into a design, or tubes that form a triangle—acting on coil springs that are usually concealed, but sometimes visible.

Stepped seat: Also known as a "King and Queen" seat, it positions the passenger high above the rider, and was a defining element of choppers from the '60s and '70s.

Tires: Only the rear tire is mentioned because it's the one that varies the most in width. Most standard Harley-Davidsons come with rear tires that are 130-150 mm wide—about five to six inches. Some choppers have rear tires that are 300 mm wide (nearly the width of two pages of this book!), and recently, a company began offering a 360-mm tire.

Transmissions: Those built by aftermarket companies sometimes come with their final-drive sprockets or pulleys on the right side rather than the normal left-side placement. This is usually done in order to accommodate a very wide rear tire. (See *Tires.*) Most are conventional foot-shift transmissions with a hand-operated clutch, but some—as noted in the specification chart—are fitted with hand shifters and foot clutches, which were commonly used on motorcycles prior to the early 1950s.

Triple trees, or trees: Formed pieces that hold the fork legs, connecting them to the handlebars and frame neck. Some are designed to add more rake to the forks than is provided by the frame neck.

Wheels: Range from spoke-type that are relatively common and inexpensive, to one-off designs intricately milled from a solid disk of metal that can cost thousands of dollars apiece. In our specification charts, the latter usually include the supplier's name.